CHEF DANIEL BOULUD

COOKING IN NEW YORK CITY

Thank you to Duggal Visual Solutions,
3 West 20th Street, New York, New York
for contributing film and processing to the project.

Assouline Pubishing, Inc.
601 West 26th Street,
18th floor
New York, NY 10001, USA
Tel: 212 989-6810   Fax: 212 647-0005
www.assouline.com

ISBN: 2 84323 370 4

Proofread by Kate Nintzel and Rebecca Nance

Color separation: Gravor (switzerland)
Printed by Grafiche Milani (Italy).

DANIEL BOULUD AND PETER KAMINSKY

CHEF DANIEL BOULUD

COOKING IN NEW YORK CITY

• 75 RECIPES •

PHOTOGRAPHS BY MARTIN H. M. SCHREIBER
AND HERVE AMIARD

ASSOULINE

*To my wife, Micky, and my daughter, Alix
and*

*To all the cooks, stewards, waitstaff, office staff and managers
who have dedicated themselves to my three restaurants
—Daniel Boulud*

*To Melinda, Lucy and Lily
—Peter Kaminsky*

6:00 a.m.	*First Light • From Pennsylvania to Périgord*
6:30 a.m.	Bread and Pastry Production • Deliveries Arrive
7:00 a.m.	Kitchen Preparation Begins for Lunch at Café Boulud and db Bistro Moderne
7:30 a.m.	Florist Set up
8:00 a.m.	Cleaning Crew Arrives
8:30 - 10:00 a.m.	*To Market*: Fish; Shellfish; Vegetables; Meat
10:00 a.m.	Kitchen Preparation Begins for Dinner at Daniel
11:00 a.m.	Post-Market Snack • *Sweet Aromas*
11:30 a.m.	Staff Meals at Café Boulud and db Bistro Moderne
12:00 p.m.	*Lunch* db Bistro Moderne/Café Boulud *The Melting Pot*
1:00 p.m.	Robert Parker and Friends Wine Lunch
2:00 p.m.	Waiters and Front of House Staff Arrive Set up of the Dining Rooms
3:00 p.m.	*Desire in a Bottle*
4:00 p.m.	We Eat First: Staff Meal at Daniel
4:30 p.m.	Citymeals-on-Wheels Event at Rockefeller Center
5:00 p.m.	Feasts & Fêtes: Catering at the Metropolitan Museum of Art
5:30 p.m.	*All is Ready*
6:00 p.m.	*Dinner Service* • Dinner at Daniel Cocktails • Bellecour Room
7:00 p.m.	The Heat Rises
8:00 p.m.	The Tasting Menu: 16 dishes, 8 courses, 9 wines
11:00 p.m.	Late Night Chefs Dinner • *Winding Down*
1:00 a.m.	Out on the Town

Recipe Contents

First Light

St. Pierre de Chandieu is a tiny dot of a hamlet in the countryside of Lyon, barely a town: two boulangeries, one pharmacy and a small church. It has only two things in common with Manhattan. One is the quiet just before dawn when the air is cool and sweet and the world so still that even in the great city you can hear the morning calls of songbirds.

Soon, though, New York will wake to the roar of trucks, the rumble of trains underground, the impatient blare of taxi horns, the clack-clack of heels on concrete, the friendly yet profane calls of deliverymen. Likewise, in the rolling hills of the French farm town, the sounds of a wakening world tickle the ears of the early-rising farmer out doing chores: bleat of lamb, cry of rooster, lowing of cow, the whisper of the wind falling off the slopes of the Alps, moving through the vineyards and the fields of wheat and corn.

The sun comes up full. The big city and the little farm village go their separate ways. But they will continue to share something all through the day: In the city that never sleeps there is a chef who barely sleeps: a bespectacled dynamo who speaks rock-and-roll slang with a thick Lyonnaise accent and who serves forth exquisite renditions of French country fare alongside modern fantasies of global cuisine.

6:00 a.m.

With three restaurants—one a sweeping palace on Manhattan's
grand boulevard, Park Avenue, one a cozy neighborhood hangout
in the fanciest district in town and one a modern bistro in the
frantic heart of Times Square—Daniel Boulud is one of the reigning
restaurateurs of New York, a chef at the height of his powers and
peak of his fame. Daniel, citizen of St. Pierre de Chandieu, Manhattan
and the world of haute cuisine.

From Pennsylvania to Périgord

In the French countryside, a great restaurant often has a garden out back, farmers down the road, a lucky huntsman or fisherman or two in the fields and streams, a neighborhood baker as round as a Botero sculpture and local produce as varied and deeply flavored as any on earth. Likewise, the country near New York City is blessed with deep black topsoil that yields strawberries resembling dark rubies, potatoes as silky as fresh cream, green beans with the snap of a fresh breeze and lettuce as lacy as rime ice.

The New York shoreline nourishes oysters, lobsters, clams, mussels and scallops, all of them briny, white and sweet. Offshore, the waters of the Atlantic shelf teem with striped bass, flounder and sole, as well as the best and rarest tuna. All up and down the Eastern seaboard, small-scale farmers grow to order for the demanding diners of Gotham: milk-fed poultry, baby lambs, pigs that eat only apples, free-range beef.

If something isn't available locally, the top restaurants will pay to have it flown or shipped from wherever it is available. Truffles from Périgord—at $450 per pound they are a bargain compared to the $1900 that the white truffles of Alba fetch. Loup de mer travels across the Atlantic, kept quietly alive in nearly freezing water.

Langoustines from Denmark, winter cherries from Chile, baby eels from the Caribbean, cheeses from the Jura Mountains, star anise lemon grass and fish sauce from Saigon. More ingredients from more places in the world arrive in New York every day than any other city on earth.

Now, at the beginning of the day, the fish, shellfish, vegetables and meat arrive at Daniel's three restaurants. A driver pulls up from Pennsylvania with a consignment of milk-fed chickens and a box of Krispy Kreme donuts. The early shift at the restaurant receives the former and chows down on the latter. Coffee in cardboard cups, a quick cigarette, two bites of a donut, conversation about the weather, sports, girlfriends. Prices are higher than they used to be, say the restaurant workers. Not where they should be, counters the chicken farmer. It all depends on your point of view. To the chicken, though, it doesn't make much difference. She is minutes away from the pot as the first fires of the day warm the quiet kitchen. And tonight she'll end up with slivers of truffle on her breast.

6:30 a.m.

Knead

Bread Production

Mix

Roll

Bake

Smell

Garlic Focaccia

Makes two 9- to 10-inch focaccia

- 2 teaspoons coarse cornmeal
- 1 head garlic, cut in half crosswise
- 2 1/2 tablespoons extra-virgin olive oil
- 1 teaspoon active dry yeast
- 1 1/2 cups warm water (95°-100°F)
- 4 cups bread flour
- 1 tablespoon fine sea salt
- 1 1/2 teaspoons sugar
- 1 teaspoon coarse sea salt
- 1/4 cup freshly grated Parmesan cheese
- 1 sprig thyme, leaves only

1. Center a rack in the oven and preheat the oven to 375°F. Line a baking sheet with parchment paper, sprinkle with the cornmeal and keep nearby.

2. Drizzle the cut sides of the garlic with 1 tablespoon of olive oil. Place cut side down on the prepared baking sheet. Bake until the cloves are so tender (but not mushy) they can be popped out of their peels with just the slightest pressure, about 1 hour. Cool to room temperature.

3. Combine the yeast, water, flour, remaining 1 1/2 tablespoons olive oil, salt and sugar in the bowl of an electric mixer fitted with the dough hook attachment. Mix on low speed until the dough comes together, about 3 minutes.

4. Increase the speed to high and mix for 8 to 10 minutes. (Keep an eye on your mixer since it may shake a bit on the counter as the dough becomes more elastic.)

5. Stop the mixer and check the dough: Grease your fingers with butter or olive oil and pull off a small piece of dough. Stretch the dough between your fingers: It should be shiny, elastic and smooth and should not break apart. You can also check the inside of the mixer bowl: The sides will be clean when the dough is ready. If the dough is not elastic enough, mix it for a few more minutes and check again.

6. Use your hands to form the dough into a ball and place it in a lightly greased large bowl. Cover with lightly greased plastic wrap and let the dough rise in a warm, draft-free area until the dough increases to 1 1/2 times its original size, approximately 1 hour.

7. Turn the dough out onto a lightly floured work surface and cut into two equal pieces. To form each focaccia, grab part of the outside edge of the dough between your forefinger and thumb and pull it into the center. Press down firmly and give the dough a quarter turn. Repeat until you have made about three full 360° turns (or 12 quarter turns). Turn the dough over. At this point, the dough should be round and the outer skin should be sufficiently stretched but not broken. This shaping process is important and will ensure an even form later. Place the balls on a lightly floured baking sheet, cover loosely with plastic wrap and let rest for approximately 1 1/2 hours.

8. Place a rack in the lowest part of the oven and preheat the oven to 475°F.

9. Use your hands to gently press the air out of the balls of dough, using more pressure around the edges to taper them slightly. The focaccia should be about 9 to 10 inches in diameter. Use a single-edged razor blade or a sharp thin knife to slash the dough at a 45° angle, no more than 1/2-inch deep, in a criss cross pattern, leaving about 1 1/2 inches between each cut. Brush the focaccia with the remaining tablespoon of olive oil and then sprinkle with the coarse salt and Parmesan cheese. Stud the focaccia with the roasted garlic cloves and gently press in the thyme leaves.

10. Use a spray bottle to generously mist the breads with water. Transfer the baking sheet to the oven and spray the bottom of the oven with several tablespoons of water. (The steam generated will help the breads form a nice crust.) Bake until the focaccia are golden brown, approximately 15 to 20 minutes. Remove from the oven and cool the breads on a wire rack.

Olive oil, roasted garlic, Parmesan and thyme

What Mark Fiorentino, the baker, and I try to do at Daniel is create a good balance between the food and the bread. Our goal is to create bread that is interesting enough on its own to be a wonderful experience. A baker really has to have a great touch. There's no margin for error. Since bread has only three or four ingredients, the balance has to be just right, especially in classic combinations such as sweet garlic and Parmesan foccacia or wheat bread with kalamata olives and rosemary. Bakers are like poets. Out of a very few and simple ingredients they make something soul nourishing.—DB

Olive Rosemary Bread

Makes 2 boules

- 2 1/4 teaspoons active dry yeast, about 1 packet
- 1 1/3 cups warm water (95° to 100° F)
- 4 1/2 cups bread flour
- 1 tablespoon wheat bran
- 1 tablespoon salt
- 1/2 teaspoon sugar
- 1/4 teaspoon freshly ground black pepper
- 1/4 cup extra-virgin olive oil
- 1 1/2 cups kalamata olives, pitted and halved
- 2 sprigs rosemary, leaves removed and finely chopped

1. In the bowl of a mixer fitted with the dough hook attachment, combine the yeast, water, flour, wheat bran, salt, sugar, pepper and oil. Mix on low speed until the dough comes together, approximately 2 to 3 minutes.

2. Increase the speed to high and mix for 8 to 10 minutes. (Keep an eye on your mixer since it may shake a bit on the counter as the dough becomes more elastic.)

3. Stop the mixer and check the dough: Grease your fingers with butter or olive oil and pull off a small piece of dough. Stretch the dough between your fingers: It should be shiny, elastic and smooth and should not break apart. You can also check the inside of the mixer bowl: The sides will be clean when the dough is ready. If the dough is not elastic enough, mix it for a few more minutes and check again.

4. Add the chopped olives and rosemary and mix on slow speed for another 3 minutes. Any olives remaining in the bowl can be worked into the dough by hand.

5. Use your hands to form the dough into a ball and place it in a lightly greased mixing bowl. Cover with lightly greased plastic wrap and let the dough rise in a warm, draft-free area until the dough increases to 1 1/2 times its original size (about 1 1/2 hours).

6. Turn the dough out onto a lightly floured work surface and cut into 2 equal pieces. To form each boule, grab part of the outside edge of the dough between your forefinger and thumb and pull it into the center. Press down firmly and give the dough a quarter turn. Repeat until you have made about three full 360° turns (or 12 quarter turns). Turn the dough over. At this point, the dough should be round and the outer skin should be sufficiently stretched but not broken. This shaping process is important and will ensure an evenly shaped boule. Place the balls, seam side down, on a lightly floured baking sheet, cover loosely with plastic wrap and let rest for approximately 1 1/2 hours.

7. Arrange racks on the lower and upper third of the oven and preheat the oven to 475°F. Line a baking sheet with parchment paper and sprinkle with cornmeal.

8. Gently transfer the dough to the prepared baking sheet. Using a single-edged razor blade or a sharp thin knife held at a 45° angle, cut 3 parallel slits 1/2-inch deep and 1 1/2 inches apart on each ball.

9. Use a spray bottle to generously mist the dough with water. Transfer the pan to the lower rack in the oven and spray the bottom of the oven with several tablespoons of water. (The steam generated will help the breads form a nice crust.) Bake for approximately 30 minutes. Reduce the heat to 375°F, move the breads to the top rack and continue baking until the breads are a dark golden brown and sound hollow when tapped, about 10 minutes. Remove from the oven and cool on a wire rack.

kalamata olives, rosemary and wheat

Lemon Yogurt Cake

Makes 1 loaf

- 3 lemons
- 1/2 cup plus 2 tablespoons plain whole yogurt
- 1 cup plus 2 tablespoons sugar
- 2 large eggs
- 1/2 cup vegetable oil
- Finely grated zest of 1 orange
- 1/2 vanilla bean, split and scraped
- 1 cup plus 2 tablespoons all-purpose flour
- 2 1/4 teaspoons baking powder

1. Center a rack in the oven and preheat the oven to 350°F. Butter the inside of a 9- by 5- by 2 1/2-inch loaf pan, dust with flour and tap out the excess.

2. Finely grate the zest of the lemons; juice 2 of the lemons. In a large bowl, whisk together the yogurt, sugar and eggs. Add the vegetable oil, lemon zest and juice, orange zest and vanilla bean seeds. Add the flour and baking powder, whisking just until combined. Do not overmix.

3. Pour the batter into the prepared pan. Bake until a knife inserted into the center of the cake comes out clean, 50 to 60 minutes. The cake will be dark golden brown on top and should pull away just a bit from the sides of the pan. If the crust begins to darken too much, cover the cake with a piece of aluminum foil. Cool in the pan on a wire rack for 10 minutes. Invert the cake onto a wire rack, remove the pan and cool completely.

Chocolate Cherry Bread

Makes 2 loaves

- 1 2/3 cups dried cherries
- 2/3 cup Kirsch
- 6 3/4 teaspoons (3/4 ounce) active dry yeast
- 1 1/3 cups warm water (95° to 100° F)
- 3 2/3 cups all-purpose flour
- 6 tablespoons unsalted butter
- 1/2 cup sugar
- 1 1/2 tablespoons salt
- 6 tablespoons cocoa powder
- 1 2/3 cups chopped semi-sweet, milk or dark chocolate
- 1 egg, lightly beaten

1. Place the cherries in a small pot and add enough water to cover them. Bring to a boil and drain. In a small bowl, combine the cherries and Kirsch and let marinate overnight.

2. Combine the yeast and water and stir until the yeast is dissolved. Mix in 1 cup of the flour and work out any lumps with your fingers. Let sit for 1 hour in a warm, draft-free area.

3. Transfer the dough to the bowl of a mixer fitted with the dough hook attachment. Add the remaining 2 2/3 cups flour, butter, sugar and salt. Mix on low speed until the dough comes together, approximately 2 to 3 minutes.

4. Increase the speed to high and mix for 8 to 10 minutes. (Keep an eye on your mixer as it will shake a bit on the counter.)

5. Stop the mixer and check the dough: Grease your fingers with butter and pull off a small piece of dough. Stretch the dough between your fingers: It should be shiny, elastic and smooth and should not break apart. You can also check the inside of the mixer bowl: The sides should be clean when the dough is ready. If the dough is not elastic enough, mix it for a few more minutes and check again.

6. Add the cocoa powder and mix for 1 to 2 minutes. Add the cherries, chocolate and any remaining Kirsch liquid and mix on slow speed for another 3 minutes. Any cherries and chocolate remaining in the bowl can be worked into the dough by hand.

7. Use your hands to form the dough into a ball and place it in a lightly greased mixing bowl. Cover with lightly greased plastic wrap and let the dough relax for approximately 1 hour in a warm, draft-free area

8. Turn the dough out onto a lightly floured work surface and cut into 2 equal pieces. To form each loaf, gently shape each piece into a rough square, approximately 5 by 5 inches. Fold down the top third of the dough to the center of the square. Using the heels of your hands, press the dough together. Turn the dough 180° and repeat. Turn the dough 180° and fold the dough in half by bringing the top edge down to meet the bottom edge. Using the heels of your hands, press the edges together. Roll the dough into a log the length of the loaf pan.

8. Spray two 9- by 5- by 3-inch metal loaf pans with nonstick cooking spray. Transfer the dough to the prepared pans, seam side down, and press the dough into the pan until it is slightly flattened and covers the bottom of the pan. Cover the pans loosely with lightly greased plastic wrap and let the dough rise for approximately 2 1/2 hours in a warm, draft-free area until the dough increases to 1 1/2 times its original size.

9. Meanwhile, arrange a rack on the lowest position of the oven and preheat the oven to 400° F.

10. Brush the top of each loaf with the beaten egg. Place the pans in the oven and spray the bottom of the oven with several tablespoons of water. (The steam generated will help the breads form a nice crust.) Bake the breads until they are dark brown and sound hollow when tapped, approximately 35 to 45 minutes. If the crust begins to darken too much, cover with a piece of aluminum foil. Remove the pans from the oven and let the bread sit in the pans for 10 minutes.

At the restaurant, we also eat this bread warm with chocolate ice cream.

A good pastry chef needs to have an artistic eye and touch as well as a great palate. Visually, pastries are an art form. What makes them exciting is the chef's combination of texture, taste and form. In a tiny chocolate, the combination of taste might be a crunchy nougatine on the outside, then a layer of bitter ganache, then framboise on the inside. First you get the crunch, then the bitter chocolate, then the sweet fruit. It's an unbelievable combination—rich, buttery, fruity—it's concentrated texture and pleasure. —DB

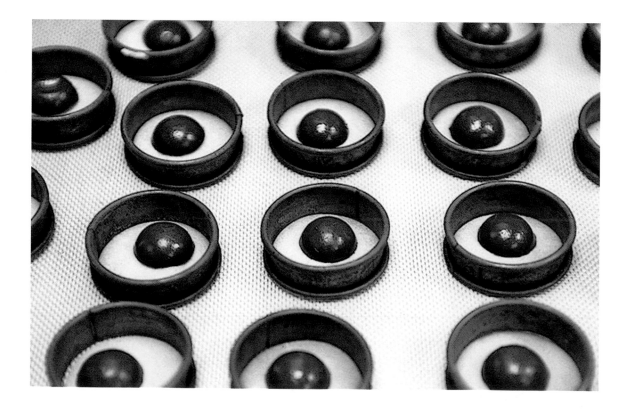

Recipe for a Perfect Bouquet

Ingredients:

- 3 large philodendron leaves
- 10 phormium leaves
- 2 bunches red dogwood branches
- 1 bale smoke bush branches, stems cut on an angle with pruning shears and split vertically up the stem
- 100 stems Sarah Bernhardt Peonies
- 100 stems Dr. Alexander Fleming Peonies (Stems should be cleaned of lower leaves, cut at a 45 degree angle with a florist's knife and placed in tepid water mixed with cut-flower food at least one day ahead of time to ensure proper absorption.)
- 4 bunches barker bush

Tools Needed:

- Pruning shears
- Florist's knife
- 2 tall glass cylinder vases (approximately 20 inches high and 8 inches in diameter)
- 1 medium glass cylinder vase (approximately 10 inches high and 9 inches in diameter)
- Scissors
- Green raffia

Instructions:

1. Place the 3 cylinder vases approximately 1 foot apart on a long and narrow console (the smaller vase should go in the center). Fill each vase halfway with tepid water.

2. To cover the vases, cut the stem of each philodendron leaf on a 45 degree angle, retaining most of the height and place one leaf into each of the vases. Carefully fold the leaf in half, exposing its underside, and wrap it around the base of the cylinder. Tie in place with raffia and cover the raffia with a knotted phormium leaf.

3. Place one bunch red dogwood branches into each of the larger cylinders and bend them in front of the smaller vase until they meet. Tie the bunches together with raffia and a phormium leaf.

4. Starting with the larger vases, arrange most of the smoke bush branches into the back of each vase to achieve a cloud-like design. Be sure to leave space for the peonies. Next, place about 40 stems of peonies at varying heights in front of the smoke bush. Insert 1 bunch barker bush in front of the peonies to frame your design. The leaves of the barker bush should cascade out of the vase.

5. Repeat step 4 for the center vase, using the rest of the peonies and barker bush, filling in where necessary. Fill each vase with tepid water and mist the peonies daily.

L'Olivier Floral Atelier's Favorite Bouquet Combinations

- Sunflowers, lemons and rosemary
- Jade Green roses, lady's mantel and ornithogalum arabicum
- White dogwood branches, lime green viburnum and white French tulips
- Large Mango Calla lilies with lily grass
- White Cymbidium orchids, horsetail and philodendron

7:30 a.m.

A restaurant is an extension of one's home, and we take as much care and pride in cleaning as we do in cooking and serving. The details of cleaning the restaurant and kitchen are as involved as all the minutiae of food preparation. Imagine throwing a party at your home every night for 200 people! —DB

To Market

A great meal starts in the market. Every young chef learns this before he dices his first onion. What looks good and what appeals to the senses varies from day to day and place to place. There may be frost in the Catskills or hail on the Delaware—the fate of natural products hangs on nature's whims. The marketplace tells the record of those events more surely than any written chronicle.

When Daniel started as a young apprentice at the age of fourteen in Lyon's Restaurant Nandron, he would go to the town market.

Early each morning, all the great chefs—Bocuse, Troisgros, Chapel, Vacombe—were there picking over the best of the day, hanging out with the other members of the restaurant family, drinking coffee, trading gossip, even letting the young kid listen in.

Ideas are born in the market. An ingredient will speak to the chef, demanding in some natural, nonverbal language that it be served up. Ingredients at their peak fairly beg to be prepared. The chef feels this. Tonight's specials—the serendipitous creations that surprise and delight chef and diner alike—will somehow come out of the alchemic reaction of chefly inspiration and raw material.

Boulud was schooled in three great restaurants that transformed French dining in the 1970s. His first lesson was in the reworked traditional food that came from the kitchen of Georges Blanc. Raised on the vibrant and hearty grand-mère cuisine of the Rhone Valley, Blanc lightened, refined and deepened the flavors of a rich culinary heritage. Next, Daniel studied at the Provençal kitchen of Roger Vergé where Mediterranean ingredients—sunny, light and clean on the palate—overtook the heavier Parisian cuisine that was the only French food many gourmets knew. And finally, in the southwest, Daniel learned the ineffably light, imaginative and simple creations of Michel Guérard.

Daniel Boulud's time in New York coincides with the American dining revolution that was born in the markets and restaurants of California in the late 1970s. By the time Boulud arrived in the United States in 1981, greenmarkets featuring the best local fare and hard-to-find heirloom products were beginning to reshape the face of New York dining. Fancy was no longer good enough. Creativity and the gastronomic signature of a chef came into demand.

Newly food-conscious America was ready for Boulud. Within two years of working in the private dining room of the EEC in Washington and the hotels Westbury and Plaza Athénée in New York, Daniel was anointed by Sirio Maccioni to take the helm at café society's beloved Le Cirque.

It was a hugely fortunate coming together of a sea change in dining: A clientele who could afford anything, a restaurateur who would do whatever it took to please and tantalize and, in Daniel, a young chef coming into the fullness of his talent and given free reign to cook anything he could dream up.

Le Cirque in the 1980s became the top restaurant in the city and, for the first time in its history, New York had a restaurant that was a global dining destination. Princes, presidents and popes; models, moguls and middle-class food lovers (who have been the largest impetus behind the fine-dining renaissance in New York) all flocked to be seen in the high-wattage boite and helped elevate Daniel to the peak of the New York dining firmament.

He has gone from Le Cirque to Restaurant Daniel on Madison Avenue and then reinstalled that restaurant in a makeover of Le Cirque's former home on Park Avenue. The new Daniel has brought diners back to the spot where he first created the home cooking of the rich, the famous or just the hopelessly foodstruck. In surroundings of quiet hip elegance, Daniel has returned to the scene of his first great triumph and now, as then, he prods the melons, sniffs the fish, tests the snap of the asparagus—and thinks about not merely what is good, but what he hopes to make memorable from today's offerings at the market.

It's common for chefs to talk about the wonderful local ingredients they use while neglecting to praise the great people from whom they get these ingredients. I'm often guilty of this too. But our relationships with our suppliers influence the way we cook. My suppliers come from many different backgrounds—many weren't farmers to begin with but made career changes later in life. They have an incredible passion for good ingredients and put a lot of care into their work. They are constantly reassessing what they grow and constantly educating themselves. I have a vegetable supplier, Tim Stark from Eckerton Hill Farm, who grows every type of tomato imaginable because he always wants to surprise us. Then there is Sylvia Pryzant, who raises pigs, chickens and ducks in Pennsylvania. She understands exactly what we need and she communicates it to the farmers around her. It's amazing. Together we've created a whole network of suppliers who provide us with all the great ingredients that America offers. —DB

Fish

I've been buying fish from Phil Rozzo for twenty years. He's a very honest man with a small shop and great fish, a very New York guy. He always listens to the chef's needs and every night he scouts the fish market to fulfill them. He's now served a couple of generations of New York chefs. He has good instincts,and for the basics—good flounder, good all-American fish—he's the best.—DB

Tuna Bagnat

Makes 4 servings

- 2 tablespoons extra-virgin olive oil
- 1/2-pound piece sushi-quality tuna (1 1/2-inches thick and 4-inches long)
- Coarse sea salt and coarsely ground black pepper
- 4 cloves garlic (3 unpeeled and lightly crushed, 1 peeled and halved)
- 4 sprigs thyme
- 2 sprigs rosemary
- One 8-inch round or square focaccia, sliced horizontally in half (see Garlic Focaccia recipe)
- Grated zest and juice of 1 lemon
- Leaves of Boston or butter lettuce, washed and dried
- 8 large basil leaves, rinsed and dried
- 2 large tomatoes, peeled, seeded and cut into quarters
- 1 ripe avocado, peeled, halved, pitted and cut lengthwise into 8 slices
- 2 stalks celery, peeled, trimmed and cut into thin diagonal slices
- 1 small seedless cucumber, peeled, halved, cut into 3-inch segments and thinly sliced lengthwise
- 10 kalamata or Provençal olives, pitted and cut in half
- 4 oil-cured anchovies, cut in half lengthwise
- 8 quail eggs, hard boiled for 4 minutes, or 2 large eggs, hard boiled for 10 minutes; peeled

1. Warm 2 tablespoons olive oil in a small sauté pan over medium-high heat. Season the tuna with salt and pepper. When the oil starts to shimmer, add the tuna, the 3 unpeeled garlic cloves, the thyme and the rosemary. Cook the tuna for 3 to 4 minutes on each side for rare, or 5 to 7 minutes on each side for medium. Remove the tuna to a plate to cool slightly. Discard the garlic and herbs.

2. Place the focaccia, cut sides up, on a work surface and brush lightly with olive oil. Rub each side of the focaccia with the cut garlic and sprinkle with salt, pepper, a pinch of the lemon zest and a few drops of lemon juice. Cover each half with the lettuce leaves.

3. Tear the basil leaves into pieces and put on top of the lettuce. Evenly place the tomatoes, avocado, celery and cucumber on each focaccia half. Season with pepper, olive oil, lemon zest and juice and distribute the olives and anchovies on top. Season the sandwich well with more pepper, olive oil and lemon zest and juice.

4. Slice the tuna lengthwise into 1/8-inch thick strips and place in rows over the vegetables on both sandwich halves; Season with more olive oil, remaining lemon zest and juice and salt and pepper. Carefully put the sandwich halves together, press firmly and wrap tightly in plastic wrap. Weigh the sandwich with a 2-pound weight and refrigerate for 3 hours. Turn the sandwich over every hour, making sure to keep the sandwich weighted.

Wine selection
- Napa Valley Rosé (U.S.)
  Joseph Phelps "Vin de Mistral" 2000

"A Blend of Grenache and Syrah, this refreshing rosé is round, juicy and light enough so as to not overwhelm this classic summer preparation "

To serve: Cut the sandwich into 4 wedges and serve with the hardboiled quail eggs, a bowl of olive oil and a dish of sea salt. Dip the eggs into the oil and salt and eat between bites of the sandwich.

Roasted Monkfish with Curried Lobster Sauce

Makes 4 servings

For the Spinach Purée:
- 2 tablespoons unsalted butter
- 1/2 large onion, finely chopped
- 1 pound spinach, stems and tough center veins removed, well washed
- Salt and freshly ground pepper

1. Heat 1 tablespoon of the butter in a large sauté pan over medium-high heat until melted and golden brown. Add the onion and cook, stirring, until it is tender but not colored, about 5 to 7 minutes. Add the spinach and cook until the spinach is tender but still bright green, about 5 minutes. Transfer to a bowl and place in the refrigerator to cool.

2. In a blender, purée the spinach mixture until smooth. In a small sauté pan, melt the remaining butter over medium heat and cook until golden brown. Stir the butter into the spinach purée and season with salt and pepper.

For the Caramelized Apples:
- 1 tablespoon sugar
- 2 tablespoons unsalted butter
- 1 Granny Smith apple, peeled, cored and cut into 8 wedges

In a large sauté pan over medium-high heat melt the sugar and cook to a light golden brown. Add the butter and apples and cook, while stirring, until the apples are evenly caramelized. Set aside and keep warm.

For the Lobster:
- Two 1 1/2-pound live lobsters, rinsed under cold water, or freshly steamed lobsters (the lobsters should be purchased and steamed the day you serve this dish)

If you are steaming the lobsters, bring a few inches of salted water to a boil in a lobster pot or stockpot. Plunge the lobsters into the pot, cover and steam them for 7 minutes. Drain. When the lobsters are cool enough to handle, remove the meat from the claws. Shell and devein the tail and cut each of the tails crosswise into medallions; reserve. Reserve the claw meat and heads.

For the Salpicon:
- 3 tablespoons extra-virgin olive oil
- 1 medium celery root, peeled and cut into 1/4-inch dice
- 2 small carrots, peeled, trimmed and cut into 1/4-inch dice
- 1 small onion, peeled, trimmed and cut into 1/4-inch dice
- Lobster claw meat, cut into 1/4-inch dice
- Salt and freshly ground pepper

In a small sauté pan over medium heat, warm 1 tablespoon of the olive oil, add the celery root and sauté until tender. Transfer to a bowl. Repeat with the carrots and onion and add to the celery root. Add the lobster claw meat and toss well. Season with salt and pepper. Set aside and keep warm.

For the Curried Lobster Sauce:
- 2 tablespoons extra-virgin olive oil
- 2 reserved lobster heads, membranes removed
- 1/2 small fennel bulb, peeled, trimmed and roughly chopped
- 1 small carrot, peeled, trimmed and roughly chopped
- 1 small onion, peeled, trimmed and roughly chopped
- 1 small stalk celery, peeled, trimmed and roughly chopped
- 2 sprigs thyme
- 2 cloves garlic, peeled and roughly chopped
- 1 tablespoon tomato paste
- 1 teaspoon Madras curry powder
- Pinch of saffron

- 1/2 cup dry vermouth
- 1/2 cup cognac or brandy
- About 4 cups unsalted chicken stock or store-bought low-sodium chicken broth
- 1/2 cup heavy cream
- 2 tablespoons unsalted butter
- Salt and freshly ground pepper

1. In a large pan over medium-high heat, warm the olive oil. Add the lobster heads, fennel, carrot, onion, celery, thyme and garlic and cook for about 5 minutes. Add the tomato paste, curry powder and saffron. Cook for another 2 minutes.
2. Add the vermouth and cognac. Flambé and cook until all of the alcohol has evaporated. Add enough stock to cover the heads. Bring the mixture to a boil, reduce the heat and let simmer for 1 hour. Pass the mixture through a fine-mesh sieve into a medium pot. Add the heavy cream and let the sauce reduce by one-half until it is thick and creamy. Stir in the butter and season with salt and pepper.

For the Monkfish:
- 2 tablespoons Madras curry powder
- 2 tablespoons all-purpose flour
- Four 6-ounce monkfish fillets, with the skin left on, cut in half
- 4 tablespoons unsalted butter
- 2 sprigs thyme
- 2 cloves garlic, peeled and crushed
- Salt and freshly ground pepper

1. Combine the curry powder and flour and use to coat the flesh side of the fillets.
2. In a large sauté pan, melt the butter with the thyme and garlic over medium-high heat. Slip in two of the fish fillets, flesh side down, and season with salt and pepper. Cook for 3 to 4 minutes. Turn the fillets over and continue cooking until done, about 2 minutes. Remove to a plate and keep warm. Repeat with the remaining two fillets.

To Serve:
- 2 tablespoons unsalted butter
- 1 tablespoon finely chopped Italian parsley

Reheat the lobster medallions with the butter and parsley in a large saute pan over medium heat just until warm. Spoon the spinach puree onto the center of each plate. Place the fillets on top. Place two lobster medallions, a spoonful of the salpicon and the caramelized apples around the fish. Spoon the curried lobster sauce around the dish.

Wine selection
- Anderson Valley Gewurztraminer, California (U.S.) Navarro 2000

66 This dry Gewurztraminer, one of the better ones in the U.S., has enough character to stand its ground with this dish while the union of the curry and the rose petal aromas of the wine is a happy one. 99

Cured Sardines

Makes 6
appetizer servings

- Two 26-ounce containers coarse sea salt
- 1 1/2 pounds sardine fillets, skin left on
- 2 1/2 cups white wine vinegar, plus additional if needed
- Finely grated zest of 2 lemons
- 4 cloves garlic, peeled and finely chopped
- 2 tablespoons fresh thyme leaves, finely chopped
- 2 tablespoons finely chopped Italian parsley leaves
- Salt and freshly ground pepper
- 5 cups extra-virgin olive oil, plus additional if needed

1. Spread the sea salt in an 1/8-inch thick layer in a sheet pan. Arrange the sardines in a single layer, skin side up, and cover with another layer of sea salt. Let cure for 10 minutes.

2. Gently brush the salt off the fillets and rinse in a bowl of cold water. (The skin is very fragile and will tear with too much handling.) Remove the salt from the sheet pan and line with parchment paper. Arrange the sardines in a single layer, skin side up; add enough vinegar to cover. Let cure for 20 minutes. Gently rinse the fillets in a bowl of cold water. Drain the sardines in a single layer, skin side up, on several layers of paper towels.

3. In a small bowl, combine the lemon zest, garlic, thyme and parsley and set aside. Cut out two 9- by 12-inch pieces of parchment paper. Using a 9- by 12-inch baking dish, sprinkle one-third of the garlic mixture on the bottom of the dish and season with salt and pepper. Arrange one-third of the sardines in a single layer on top of the garlic mixture and season with salt and pepper. Add enough olive oil to cover. Top with a piece of parchment paper, (this helps in the removal of the sardines from the container). Repeat this process two more times. Refrigerate 48 hours before serving.

Wine selection
- Vin de Pays de l'Hérault (France)
  Mas Jullien "Les Cailloutis" 1999

66 This sardine preparation is quite assertive and needs a wine rich enough to stand up to it. This wine, a blend of Chenin Blanc, Grenache, Petit Manseng and Viognier, is powerful yet refined with white fruit aromas. 99

we serve the

sardines

with Meyer lemon confit

vinaigrette,

garlic croutons,
toasted pine nuts
and an arugula,
mache and

frisee salad

seasoned with
lemon vinaigrette.

Potato Salad with Smoked Beluga Sturgeon & Caviar Vinaigrette

Makes 4 appetizer servings

For the Mayonnaise (makes 2/3 cup):
- 1 large egg yolk
- 1 tablespoon Dijon mustard
- 2 teaspoons freshly squeezed lemon juice
- 1 teaspoon sherry vinegar
- Salt and freshly ground pepper
- 1/2 cup grapeseed or vegetable oil

In a medium bowl, whisk together the egg yolk, mustard, lemon juice and vinegar; season with salt and pepper. Whisking constantly, add the oil in droplets. When the mixture starts to thicken, drizzle in the oil in a slow, steady stream.

For the Potato Salad:
- 1 1/2 pounds Fingerling potatoes
- 6 tablespoons Mayonnaise (see recipe above)
- 3 tablespoons crème fraîche or sour cream
- 1 shallot peeled and finely chopped
- 1 teaspoon chives, finely chopped
- Salt and freshly ground pepper

1. Place the potatoes in a large pot of salted water and bring to a boil over high heat. Cook until tender and easily pierced with a knife, about 12 to 15 minutes; drain. Peel the potatoes once they are cool enough to handle. Cool completely and cut into 1/4-inch thick slices.
2. In a large bowl, combine the Mayonnaise and crème fraîche. Add the potatoes, shallot and chives and gently toss to combine. Season with salt and pepper.

Wine selection
- Eau de Vie de Baie de Houx (France) Jean-Paul Métté

“ Made from hollyberry leaves in Alsace, this brandy is very dry with floral overtones and cuts easily through the smokiness of the dish. ”

For the Caviar Vinaigrette:
- 2 tablespoons Mayonnaise (see recipe above)
- 1 tablespoon crème fraîche or sour cream
- 2 teaspoons champagne
- 2 teaspoons Sevruga caviar
- 1/2 teaspoon sherry vinegar
- Salt and freshly ground pepper

In a small bowl, mix together all the ingredients. Season with salt and pepper

To Serve:
- 10 ounces smoked Beluga sturgeon, thinly sliced

Divide the potato salad among four plates. Arrange the sturgeon slices in a fan pattern over the potatoes and drizzle with the Caviar Vinaigrette.

Sauteed Skate

Makes 4 servings

For the Vegetables:
- 2 ounces haricot verts, ends trimmed
- 2 ounces sugar snap peas
- 2 tablespoons unsalted butter
- 8 baby turnips, peeled, tops trimmed and cut in half
- 8 baby carrots, peeled and tops trimmed
- 4 small bulb onions, tops trimmed and cut in half
- 8 small pink breakfast radishes, tops trimmed
- Salt and freshly ground pepper
- 1 cup unsalted chicken stock or store-bought low-sodium chicken broth

1. Prepare an ice-water bath in a medium bowl. Bring a large saucepan of salted water to a boil. Add the haricot verts to the boiling water and blanch until tender but still green, about 3 to 5 minutes. Use a slotted spoon to transfer them to the ice-water bath to cool. Repeat with the snap peas. Drain the vegetables and cut the haricot verts and peas in half lengthwise.
2. Melt the butter in a medium sauté pan over medium-low heat. When the pan is hot, add the turnips, carrots and onions. Sauté, stirring frequently, until the vegetables start to soften but do not brown, 3 to 5 minutes. Add the radishes, season with salt and pepper and cook for another 3 to 5 minutes. Add the stock, bring to a boil and lower the heat and reduce to a simmer. Cook until the vegetables are tender and most of the liquid has evaporated, about 15 minutes. Stir in the blanched haricot verts and peas and keep warm while preparing the skate.

For the Skate:
- 1 lemon
- 1/4 cup extra-virgin olive oil
- Four 6-ounce skate fillets, cleaned
- Salt and freshly ground pepper
- 2 tablespoons Wondra flour
- 4 tablespoons (1/2 stick) unsalted butter
- 2 plum tomatoes, peeled, seeded and cut into 1/4-inch dice
- 2 tablespoons finely chopped Italian parsley leaves
- 2 tablespoons small capers, drained
- 2 tablespoons toasted and coarsely chopped walnuts
- 2 tablespoons unsalted chicken stock or store-bought low-sodium chicken broth

1. With a paring knife, remove the peel and pith from the lemon so the flesh is exposed. Cut the lemon segments from between the membranes and cut the segments into small dice; set aside. Squeeze the membrane and reserve the juice until needed.

2. Warm 2 tablespoons of the olive oil in a large non-stick sauté pan over high heat. Season the skate fillets with salt and pepper and dust with the Wondra flour. When the oil begins to smoke, slip 2 skate fillets into the pan and cook until the fish is golden brown on one side, 2 to 3 minutes. Carefully turn the fillets over and cook until golden brown, 2 to 3 minutes. Transfer the skate to warm dinner plates. Repeat the process with the remaining olive oil and fillets.

3. Drain any remaining fat from the pan and wipe clean with a paper towel. Return the pan to high heat. Add the butter and cook until light brown, about 1 minute, before adding the diced lemon, tomatoes, parsley, capers and nuts. Cook about 1 minute before adding the stock. Bring the liquid to a boil, add the reserved lemon juice, season with salt and pepper and remove the pan from the heat.

To Serve: Spoon the sauce over the fish and arrange the vegetables on top. Serve immediately.

Wine selection
- Arbois Savagnin "En Paradis Vieilles Vignes" (France) Domaine Rickjaert 1999

❝Dry, with some light walnut aroma that echo those in the dish, this Arbois has enough body to stand up to the skate, while still being light enough for the vegetables to shine through.❞

47

Piballes story

Piballes Story

Jean-Louis Palladin, a great French chef who had a passion for *terroir*, introduced me to piballes. They are little baby eels from the southwest of France, which is where he's from. One night he got my friend Rod Mitchell to go fishing for piballes in Maine, where he was convinced they existed. They found some, and ever since we get them every spring and serve them on the tasting menu at Daniel. They come to us alive—beautiful but ephemeral since it's a very short season. We serve them the traditional Basque way: stir-fried in olive oil with garlic, a little bit of *piment d'Espelette* and some fried parsley on top. The taste is very delicate and, as they have no bones, they melt in your mouth.

My most shocking moment ever with piballes was once when I had a Japanese cook working in the kitchen. I was ready to blanch the piballes, I had them in the strainer, alive, jumping around, and he reached in and grabbed a few and gobbled them up! I couldn't believe it—for me that's like eating live worms, but for him it was the ultimate sashimi! —DB

Roasted Halibut Tail with Asparagus

Makes 8 servings

- 16 Fingerling potatoes, scrubbed (approximately 1/4 pound to 1/2 pound, depending on the size)
- 8 slices bacon
- 3 tablespoons extra-virgin olive oil
- One 3- to 4-pound halibut tail, cleaned
- Salt and freshly ground pepper
- 16 jumbo spears green asparagus, trimmed
- 16 porcini mushrooms, trimmed and cleaned (approximately 1 pound)
- 8 spring onions, white part with 1/2 inch of green
- 1 head garlic, cut crosswise in half
- 3 tablespoons unsalted butter, cut into small pieces
- 1/2 cup dry white wine
- 1 cup unsalted beef stock or store-bought low-sodium beef broth
- 2 tablespoons sherry vinegar
- 8 pieces tomato confit or drained, oil-packed sundried tomatoes
- 1 bunch wild watercress, trimmed and washed

1. Bring a large pot of salted water to a boil. Add the potatoes and cook until easily pierced with a fork, about 15 minutes. Drain.

2. Center a rack in the oven and preheat the oven to 300°F.

3. In a Dutch oven or large casserole over medium heat, cook the bacon until golden brown and crispy, about 3 minutes. Transfer to a plate lined with paper towels and drain. Cut each slice of bacon into thirds and reserve until needed.

4. Drain the bacon fat from the pot and wipe clean with a paper towel. Return the pan to medium-high heat and add the olive oil. Season the fish with salt and pepper. Slip in the halibut tail, brown skin side down, and cook for 5 minutes. Flip the fish over and add the potatoes, asparagus, mushrooms, onions and garlic; slide the pan into the oven. After 15 minutes, dot the top of the fish with the butter. The fish should be basted regularly from this point on. After 10 minutes, deglaze with the wine and continue roasting until the liquid is reduced by half, another 5 minutes. Add the stock, sherry vinegar and tomato confit and roast another 5 minutes. Remove the pan from the oven, discard the garlic head and top with the watercress. Taste and season with salt and pepper, if necessary.

To Serve: Serve family-style right from the pan.

Wine selection
- Willamette Valley Pinot Noir, Oregon (U.S.)
  Willakenzie Estate "Coleman" 1998

❝ This is a "meaty" preparation of a firm, yet moist fish that calls for a red wine. This classically styled Oregon Pinot Noir with dark cherry aromas and an earthy yet satiny finish, makes the fish even more succulent while echoing some of the porcinis' aromas. ❞

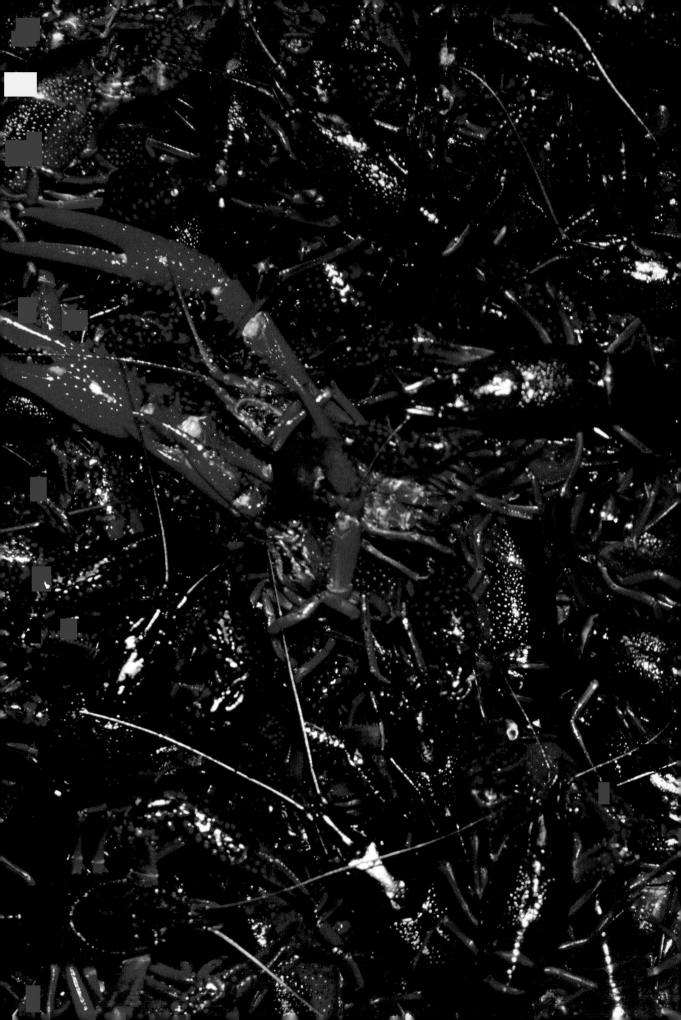

Shellfish.

With shellfish, it's all about freshness—it must be alive up until the very last minute. For me, the best shellfish is from the coast of Maine. I love the New England and north Atlantic shellfish for its brininess. Along with the shellfish from Brittany, it's the best in the world. —DB

New England Clam Chowder

Makes 4 servings

- 2 tablespoons unsalted butter
- 2 small onions: one peeled and sliced; one peeled and cut into 1/4-inch dice
- 1 teaspoon crushed red pepper flakes
- 2 sprigs thyme
- 2 pounds razor clams scrubbed and rinsed well
- 2 pounds littleneck clams scrubbed and rinsed well
- 2 pounds mahogany clams scrubbed and rinsed well
- 2 cups dry white wine
- 3 large Yukon Gold potatoes, about 2 pounds, peeled and cut into 1/2-inch dice
- 1 cup whole milk
- 1 cup heavy cream
- 2 cloves garlic, peeled and crushed
- 1/4 pound slab bacon, cut into 1/4-inch dice
- 2 medium leeks, white and light green parts, sliced
- 2 stalks celery, peeled, trimmed and cut into 1/4-inch dice
- Salt and freshly ground black pepper
- 1 tablespoon finely chopped Italian parsley leaves

1. Melt the butter in a large pot over medium heat. Add the sliced onion and cook, stirring frequently, until tender but not colored, 8 to 10 minutes. Increase the heat to high, add the pepper flakes, 1 thyme sprig, razor clams and wine. Cover with a lid and steam until the razor clams open, about 4 minutes. Using a slotted spoon or tongs, remove the razor clams and set aside. Repeat with the littleneck and then the mahogany clams. Strain the poaching liquid through several layers of cheesecloth lining a sieve to remove the sediment; set aside the poaching liquid and discard the vegetables.

2. When the clams are cool enough to handle, remove the meat and discard the shells. Refrigerate the littleneck and mahogany clams. Cut the tip off the body of the razor clams and discard. Thinly slice the remaining pencil-like body portions and refrigerate.

3. In a medium saucepan, bring the potatoes, milk, heavy cream, garlic and remaining thyme sprig to a boil. Lower the heat and simmer until the potatoes are tender enough to be pierced easily with the point of a knife and the liquid is thick and creamy, 18 to 20 minutes. Using a slotted spoon, remove half the potatoes and discard the thyme. Using a blender, hand-held immersion blender or food processor, purée the remaining potatoes and liquid until smooth.

4. Warm a large stockpot over medium heat and add the bacon. Cook, stirring, just until the bacon starts to render its fat, about 8 minutes. Reduce the heat to medium-low, add the diced onion, leeks and celery and cook, stirring frequently, until the vegetables are tender, about 15 minutes. Stir in the reserved clam meat, the diced and puréed potatoes and half the reserved poaching liquid (about 2 cups). Adjust the consistency with additional poaching liquid, if needed.

Season with salt and pepper and garnish with the chopped parsley. Serve immediately.

Wine selection
- Colli Orientali del Friuli (Italy) Bastianich "Plus" 1999

66 This Tocai Friulano, with its refreshing acidity, mineral and moderate tropical fruit aromas and bone dry finish, is a nice counterpoint to the richness of the chowder and the texture of the clams. 99

Andrew Carmellini's Spaghetti

Makes 4 servings

- 6 ounces fresh peas, shelled (about 1 1/2 cups)
- 4 tablespoons (1/2 stick) unsalted butter
- 3 medium shallots, peeled, trimmed and finely chopped
- Pinch of saffron threads
- 2 sprigs thyme
- 1 clove garlic, peeled and finely chopped
- 1/4 cup dry white wine
- 3/4 cup unsalted chicken stock or store-bought low-sodium chicken broth
- 2 pounds mussels, scrubbed and de-bearded
- 2 pounds littleneck clams or cockles, washed and cleaned thoroughly
- 8 ounces spaghetti
- 1/4 pound cherry tomatoes
- 1 tablespoon finely chopped Italian parsley leaves
- Juice of 2 lemons
- 2 tablespoons extra-virgin olive oil
- Salt and freshly ground pepper

1.   Bring a medium pot of salted water to a boil. Add the peas and cook for 5 minutes. Drain the peas and hold under cold running water to cool. Set aside.
2.   Melt 2 tablespoons of the butter in a large stockpot over medium heat. Add the shallots and cook, stirring, just until translucent, about 5 minutes. Add the saffron, thyme, garlic, wine, 1/4 cup of the stock, mussels and clams; cover with a lid and increase the heat to high. Cook just until the shellfish open, 3 to 4 minutes, stirring halfway through the cooking process. Transfer the mussels and clams to a cheesecloth-lined colander set over a large bowl. Discard any unopened shells. Reserve 1/2 cup of the shellfish broth. When the shellfish are cool enough to handle, remove the meat and discard the shells.
3.   Bring a large pot of salted water to a boil. Add the spaghetti and cook until al dente, 7 to 9 minutes; drain.
4.   Heat the remaining 2 tablespoons butter in a large sauté pan over medium-high heat. Add the 1/2 cup reserved shellfish broth and the remaining 1/2 cup stock. Bring to a boil, reduce to a simmer and cook until slightly thickened, about 3 minutes. Add the peas, shellfish, spaghetti, tomatoes, parsley, lemon juice and olive oil. Season with salt and pepper. Gently toss and cook just until heated through. Serve immediately.

Wine selection
- Rias Baixas-Albariño (Spain)
  Martin Codax 2001

" Light and mineral, this bone-dry wine from northeastern Spain is the perfect medium for the seafood in this dish to express its unique flavors. "

Stuffed Squid with Piquillo Pepper Coulis

Makes 4 servings

For the Piquillo Pepper Coulis:
- 2 tablespoons extra-virgin olive oil
- 1 tablespoon chopped onion
- 1 clove garlic, peeled and chopped
- 6 piquillo peppers, seeds removed
- 2 tablespoons unsalted chicken stock or store-bought low-sodium chicken broth
- 1/2 teaspoon freshly squeezed lemon juice

Warm the olive oil in a sauté pan over medium-high heat. Add the onion and garlic and cook until tender but not colored. Add the peppers and stock and cook an additional 2 minutes. Transfer the mixture to a blender, add the lemon juice and purée until smooth. Set aside and keep warm.

For the Stuffed Squid:
- 3/4 pound Swiss chard, stems and tough center ribs removed, washed and cut into thin strips
- 10 (approximately 1 pound) small squid, cleaned with the tentacles attached
- 1/4 cup extra-virgin olive oil
- 2 tablespoons finely chopped onion
- 2 cloves garlic, peeled and finely chopped
- 1 tablespoon pine nuts
- 1/4 pound chorizo or Italian sausage, finely chopped
- 8 piquillo peppers, seeds removed and finely chopped
- 2 tablespoons finely chopped Italian parsley leaves
- 3 tablespoons fresh bread crumbs
- Salt and freshly ground pepper

1. Bring a pot of salted water to a boil, toss in the chard and blanch for 5 minutes. Drain and squeeze the leaves dry of excess water.

2. Roughly chop two of the squid, including the tentacles. Warm 2 tablespoons of the olive oil in a large sauté pan over medium-high heat. Add the onion, garlic and pine nuts and cook until the onion and garlic are tender but not colored, about 4 minutes. Reduce the heat to medium, add the chopped squid and chorizo and cook for 2 minutes. Add the chard, peppers and parsley and cook for 2 minutes more. Toss in the bread crumbs and season with salt and pepper. Let the mixture cool completely.

3. Using a spoon or a pastry bag fitted with a large, round tip, stuff each remaining squid with the filling and use a toothpick to seal shut the opening of each squid. Season with salt and pepper. Warm the remaining 2 tablespoons of the olive oil in a large sauté pan over medium-low heat. Slip the squid into the pan and cook until golden brown on all sides, approximately 5 to 7 minutes.

Serve with the piquillo pepper coulis

Wine selection
- Colline Novaresi (Italy) "I Mimo" Rosé 2001

" This slightly dry rosé wine from Piedmont plays on the sweet spiciness of the piquillo peppers while adding a fruity side to the dish. "

" Lobster *Jus*

The hallmark of a chef is his sauces. A *jus* is simply
the concentrated flavor of a particular ingredient in its
liquid form. A plain, steamed lobster served with
butter is delicious. But a lobster served with a *jus* is
flavor intensified and raised to a whole new level.
A lobster *jus* is briny; you roast lobster carcasses, add
a smoky flavor from flambéing cognac, a slightly
sweet tang from the caramelized mirepoix and the
subtle taste of whatever herbs have been used.
Every chef has his own special secret recipe for *jus*.
I love to soak it up with a piece of bread. —DB **"**

Crayfish & Stuffed Morel Fricassee

Makes 4 appetizer servings

For the Stuffed Morels:

- 2 tablespoons extra-virgin olive oil
- 12 large plus 1/2 cup morel mushrooms: trimmed, washed and dried; 1/2 cup, roughly chopped
- Salt and freshly ground pepper
- 1 ounce fresh foie gras
- 1 ounce chicken livers
- 1/2 shallot, finely chopped, rinsed and dried
- 1/2 garlic clove, peeled and finely chopped
- 1 ounce pork shoulder or finely ground pork
- 1/2 slice bacon
- 1/2 tablespoon finely chopped Italian parsley leaves
- 1 tablespoon fresh bread crumbs
- 2 cups unsalted beef stock or store-bought low sodium beef broth
- 1 tablespoon unsalted butter

1. Place the bowl and steel blade of the food processor in the refrigerator.

2. Warm 1 tablespoon of the oil in a large sauté pan over medium heat. Add the 12 large morels, season with salt and pepper and cook, stirring occasionally, until tender, about 5 minutes. Let cool.

3. Season the foie gras with salt and pepper. Set a large, heavy sauté pan over high heat and sauté the foie gras for 1 minute on each side. Drain the foie gras on a plate lined with paper towels. Lower the heat to medium-high. In the same pan, sauté the chicken livers for 2 minutes. Drain the chicken livers on the same plate as the foie gras. Reserve the fat remaining in the pan.

4. Wipe the inside of the pan clean with a paper towel and warm the remaining 1 tablespoon olive oil over medium-high heat. Add the shallot, garlic and chopped morels and cook until tender, approximately 8 to 10 minutes. Season with salt and pepper and set aside.

5. Pass the pork and bacon through a meat grinder set on the medium holes. Remove the chilled food processor bowl and blade from the refrigerator. (The refrigeration prevents the filling from becoming too warm.) Put the morels, foie gras, chicken livers, reserved fat, shallots, garlic, pork, bacon, parsley and bread crumbs into the food processor and purée until smooth. Taste and season with salt and pepper, if necessary. Pass through a fine-mesh sieve. Place the morel stuffing into a pastry bag without a tip and pipe the filling into the whole morels.

6. Center a rack in the oven and preheat the oven to 350°F.

7. In a small ovenproof saucepan, boil the stock over high heat until reduced to 2/3 cup. Stir in the butter, add the stuffed morels and season with salt and pepper. Cover the pan with aluminum foil, slide into the oven and braise for 30 minutes. Using a slotted spoon, remove the morels from the pan, set aside and keep warm. Reserve the braising liquid.

For the Crayfish:

- 8 cups water
- 1/2 carrot, peeled, trimmed and sliced
- 1/2 onion, peeled, trimmed and sliced
- 1 clove garlic, peeled
- Finely grated zest of 1/2 orange
- 1 sprig thyme
- 1 bay leaf
- 3 tablespoons coarse sea salt
- 2 tablespoons whole black peppercorns
- 1 1/2 tablespoons coriander seeds
- 1/2 teaspoon fennel seeds
- 2 1/2 cups dry white wine
- 2 cups white wine vinegar
- 24 crayfish (approximately 1 1/2 pounds), rinsed under cold running water

1. Combine the water, carrot, onion, garlic, orange zest, thyme, bay leaf, salt, peppercorns, coriander seeds and fennel seeds in a large stockpot and bring to a boil. Reduce the heat to medium and allow the bouillon to simmer for 20 minutes. Add the wine, vinegar and crayfish; bring the bouillon back up to a boil, reduce the heat to medium and let simmer for 2 minutes. Remove the pot from the heat and cool the crayfish in the water for 10 minutes. Drain; remove the crayfish and discard the cooking liquid and vegetables.

2. To peel the crayfish, twist off the heads and reserve. Peel off the top three sections of the shell, then, holding the meat in one hand and the tip of the tail in the other, squeeze the tail while pulling the meat out of the shell. The vein in the center of the crayfish should come off with the shell. If it doesn't, remove it by hand, then use your finger to rub off any yellow coral that clings to the meat. Reserve the crayfish shells, heads and meat separately.

For the Sauce:

- 2 tablespoons extra-virgin olive oil
- Reserved crayfish shells and heads (from above)
- 1 cup morel mushrooms, cleaned, trimmed and coarsely chopped
- 1 shallot, peeled, sliced, rinsed and dried
- 1 clove garlic, peeled, halved and crushed
- 2 tablespoons sherry vinegar
- 2 cups unsalted beef stock or store-bought low-sodium beef broth

To Serve: Divide the vegetables and crayfish among 4 warm dinner plates. Top with 3 stuffed morels for each plate and spoon the sauce around. Serve immediately.

- 1 sprig savory
- Salt and freshly ground pepper

Warm the olive oil in a large sauté pan over medium-high heat. Add the reserved crayfish shells and heads and cook until golden brown. Add the morels, shallot and garlic and deglaze with the sherry vinegar. Cook until the liquid in the pan has almost evaporated. Add the stock and savory, reduce the heat to low and simmer for 45 minutes, regularly skimming off the foam and any solids that rise to the surface. Taste and season with salt and pepper. Strain through a fine-mesh sieve. If the sauce is too thick, thin with the reserved morel braising liquid. Set the sauce aside and keep warm.

For the Spinach and Fava Beans:
- 1/2 pound fava beans, shelled
- 1 teaspoon unsalted butter
- 1 pound spinach, stemmed, tough center veins removed, well washed and dried
- 1 clove garlic, peeled and crushed
- Salt and freshly ground pepper

1. Prepare an ice-water bath in a small bowl and set aside. Bring a large pot of salted water to a boil. Plunge the beans into the boiling water and blanch for 2 minutes. Remove from the heat, drain and transfer to the prepared ice-water bath. Once cooled, drain and remove the skins of the fava beans. Rinse under cold water and pat dry on paper towels.

2. Melt the butter in a large sauté pan or skillet over high heat. Add the spinach and garlic and season with salt and pepper. Toss until the spinach is tender but still bright green, about 5 minutes. Discard the garlic and drain off any liquid remaining in the pan.

To Serve:
- 1 tablespoon unsalted butter
- Salt and freshly ground black pepper

Reheat the stuffed morels in the reserved braising liquid, if necessary. Separately, in a large sauté pan over medium heat, warm the sautéed morels, spinach, fava beans, crayfish meat and butter. Season with salt and pepper to taste.

Wine selection
- Chablis Grand Cru "Blanchots Reserve de l'Obédiencerie" (France) Domaine Laroche 1997

❝The meatiness of the crayfish and the buttery earthiness of the morels call for a firm yet generous, mineral wine such as this northern Burgundy Grand Cru. The wine smells of hawthorn and fresh hay and seems to bring out even more of the dish's flavors. ❞

Vegetables

Warm White Asparagus with a Poached Egg Dressing

Makes 4 appetizer servings

For the Poached Egg Dressing:
- 1 large egg in the shell
- 1 tablespoon Dijon mustard
- 1 cup peanut oil
- 1 teaspoon black truffle juice
- 1 teaspoon red wine vinegar
- 1 drop of white truffle oil (optional)

1. Bring a small pot of water to a boil. Gently slip in the egg and cook for 4 minutes to a soft boil. Remove the egg from the pot and let the egg cool under cold running water for 2 minutes. Gently peel the egg.

2. In a blender, whir together the soft-poached egg and mustard. Slowly drizzle in the peanut oil and truffle oil, if using, and finish with the truffle juice and vinegar. Blend until the dressing is light and fluffy. Refrigerate until ready to use.

For the Spring Herb Salad:
- 1 tablespoon almond oil
- 3/4 teaspoon freshly squeezed lemon juice
- Salt and freshly ground pepper
- 2 tablespoons Italian parsley leaves
- 2 tablespoons coarsely chopped chives
- 2 tablespoons celery leaves
- 2 tablespoons mâche leaves
- 2 tablespoons watercress leaves
- 2 tablespoons chervil leaves

In a medium bowl, whisk together the almond oil and lemon juice and season with salt and pepper. Add the herbs and toss to combine.

For the Crispy Croutons:
- 1 brioche
- 2 tablespoons clarified butter
- 1/2 clove garlic, peeled
- 1 tablespoon blanched sliced almonds

Trim the crusts off the brioche. Cut into 1/4-inch cubes. In a medium sauté pan, warm the butter and garlic over medium heat. Toss in the breadcubes and almonds and sauté until golden. Drain the croutons on a plate lined with paper towels. Discard the garlic.

For the White Asparagus:
- 24 large spears white asparagus, cleaned, peeled and trimmed (it is very important to peel the white asparagus from the head to the bottom of the stem)

Put a large pot of salted water up to a boil. When the water is boiling, plunge the asparagus into the pot and cook at a full boil until tender, approximately 10 minutes (it will depend on the size of the asparagus). Using a slotted spoon, gently lift the asparagus out of the pot and drain them. Place the asparagus onto a large serving platter.

Serve the asparagus with the egg dressing and arrange the salad and croutons on the side as accompaniments.

" The best asparagus can be eaten with the fingers, dipped into the dressing. White asparagus is my favorite: It's sweeter, bigger, more tender and meatier, with a unique flavor and taste. And it's mostly wild. My friend Lee Jones's white asparagus is the best—he grows it in a cornfield, and it's very sweet, almost sugary. —DB "

Wine selection
- Muscat Grand Cru "Goldert" Domaine Zind-Humbrecht 1999

" This traditional pairing of the Muscat grape with asparagus works well because this zesty wine offers a striking contrast to the richness of the brioche. "

Potato Gnocchi with Creme Fraîche & Caviar

Makes 4 servings

For the Potato Gnocchi:
- Coarse sea salt
- 2 large Idaho potatoes (approximately 1 pound), well scrubbed
- 1 small egg, lightly beaten
- 1/2 cup all-purpose flour
- 1 teaspoon grated Parmesan cheese
- 1/2 teaspoon unsalted butter, melted
- 1/2 teaspoon extra-virgin olive oil
- 1/2 teaspoon salt
- 1/4 teaspoon freshly ground pepper
- 1/2 teaspoon freshly grated lemon zest

1. Center a rack in the oven and preheat the oven to 450°F.

2. Line a baking pan with a 1/2-inch thick layer of sea salt. Prick each potato several times with a fork and place on top of the salt. Transfer the pan to the oven and bake until the potatoes are tender when pierced with a fork, 50 to 60 minutes. Remove from the oven and set aside until cool enough to handle, 5 to 10 minutes. Peel the potatoes while they are still very warm. Pass the peeled potatoes through a food mill or a potato ricer into a medium bowl.

3. In a large bowl, using a wooden spoon, gently stir the egg, flour, Parmesan cheese, butter, olive oil, salt, pepper and lemon zest into the warm potatoes until just combined, taking care not to overwork the dough. Turn the dough out onto a lightly floured work surface. Cut off 1/8 of the dough and roll into a log approximately 16 inches long and 1/2-inch thick. Cut the log into 1/2-inch pieces and place them on a lightly floured tray or plate. Repeat using the remaining dough. (The gnocchi may be refrigerated for up to 6 hours.)

For the Crème Fraîche Sauce (makes 1 cup):
- 3/4 cup unsalted chicken stock or store-bought low-sodium chicken broth
- 4 fresh oysters, scrubbed, meat removed, juice strained and reserved
- 2 tablespoons unsalted butter
- 1 tablespoon crème fraîche
- Juice of 1 lemon
- Salt and freshly ground pepper

In a small saucepan, bring the stock to a boil. Remove from the heat and add the oyster meat and reserved juices, butter, crème fraîche and lemon juice. Season with salt and pepper. Using a hand-held immersion blender or upright blender, purée until smooth. Set aside and keep warm.

To Serve:
- Potato Gnocchi (from recipe above)
- 1 tablespoon unsalted butter
- 2 medium leeks, white and light green parts only, cut into 1/4-inch dice
- Crème Fraîche Sauce (from recipe above)
- 1 teaspoon finely chopped chives
- 3 ounces (approximately 100 g) Sevruga or Oscetra caviar
- Grated Parmesan cheese

1. Bring a large pot of salted water to a boil. Drop all the gnocchi into the boiling water and cook until they rise to the surface, about 1 to 2 minutes. Cook 30 seconds more and drain immediately.

2. In a large sauté pan over medium heat, melt the butter. Add the leeks and cook, stirring frequently, until tender, about 4 minutes. Add the gnocchi, half of the crème fraîche sauce and the chives, stirring gently until warmed through.

3. Divide the gnocchi and sauce among four warm bowls. Using a hand-held immersion blender, mix the remaining sauce until frothy and spoon over the gnocchi.

To Serve: **Top with a dollop of caviar and sprinkle with Parmesan cheese.**

Wine selection
- Champagne (France)
  Veuve Clicquot "La Grande Dame" 1995

66 This cuvee, dominated by the Pinot Noir grape, is full bodied yet dry and supremely elegant. It stands up very well to the caviar and provides some firmness to the creaminess of the gnocchi and leeks. 99

Chilled Cranberry Bean Soup with Bacon & Parsley

Makes 4 appetizer servings

- 1 tablespoon extra-virgin olive oil
- 2 ounces slab bacon: 1 ounce cut in half and 1 ounce finely chopped
- 1/3 cup chopped carrot
- 1/3 cup chopped celery
- 1/4 cup chopped onion
- 1 small leek, white and light green parts only, chopped
- 3 1/2 cloves garlic, peeled
- Bouquet garni (4 sprigs chervil, 4 sprigs Italian parsley, 1 bay leaf, 1 sprig thyme and 6 black peppercorns, tied in cheesecloth)
- 6 cups unsalted chicken stock or store-bought low sodium chicken broth

- 1 1/2 cups shelled cranberry beans
- 1/2 cup heavy cream
- 1 teaspoon sherry vinegar
- Salt and freshly ground white pepper
- Peanut oil, for frying
- 10 large Italian parsley leaves
- 1 slice white bread
- 1 tablespoon clarified butter
- 1 tablespoon fresh black truffle, chopped (optional)

1. In a large stock pot or casserole, warm the olive oil over medium-high heat. Add the 1-ounce piece bacon and cook until the bacon is a light golden brown, about 5 minutes. Add the carrot, celery, onion, leek and 3 cloves of the garlic and cook for another 10 minutes, making sure that the vegetables do not color. Add the bouquet garni and stock, bring to a boil, lower the heat and simmer for 30 minutes. Remove the vegetables and bouquet garni with a slotted spoon. Add the cranberry beans, bring the liquid back up to a boil and simmer until the beans are tender, about 45 minutes. Let the mixture cool for 15 minutes.

2. In a small saucepan, bring the heavy cream to a boil. In several batches, in a blender or food processor, purée the soup and the hot cream together until smooth. Season with the sherry vinegar, salt and pepper. Refrigerate until cold.

3. Pour 1 to 2 inches of peanut oil into a small pot and heat the oil to 325°F, as measured on a deep-fat thermometer. Fry the parsley leaves for 30 seconds to 1 minute. Drain on a plate lined with paper towels.

4. In a sauté pan over medium high heat, cook the remaining bacon until golden brown. Drain on a plate lined with paper towels.

5. Trim the crust off the bread and cut into 1/4-inch dice. In a medium sauté pan over medium heat warm the butter. Toss in the bread cubes and the remaining 1/2 clove of garlic and sauté until golden brown. Drain the croutons on a plate lined with paper towels and discard the garlic.

To Serve: **Ladle the soup into soup bowls and garnish with the fried parsley, bacon, croutons and truffle.**

Wine selection
- Trebbiano d'Abruzzo (Italy)
  Valentini 1996

66 This chilled, thick summer soup is best matched with this medium-bodied, mineral wine from one of the most original producers in northern Italy. Its slightly nutty aromas add an extra dimension to the dish. 99

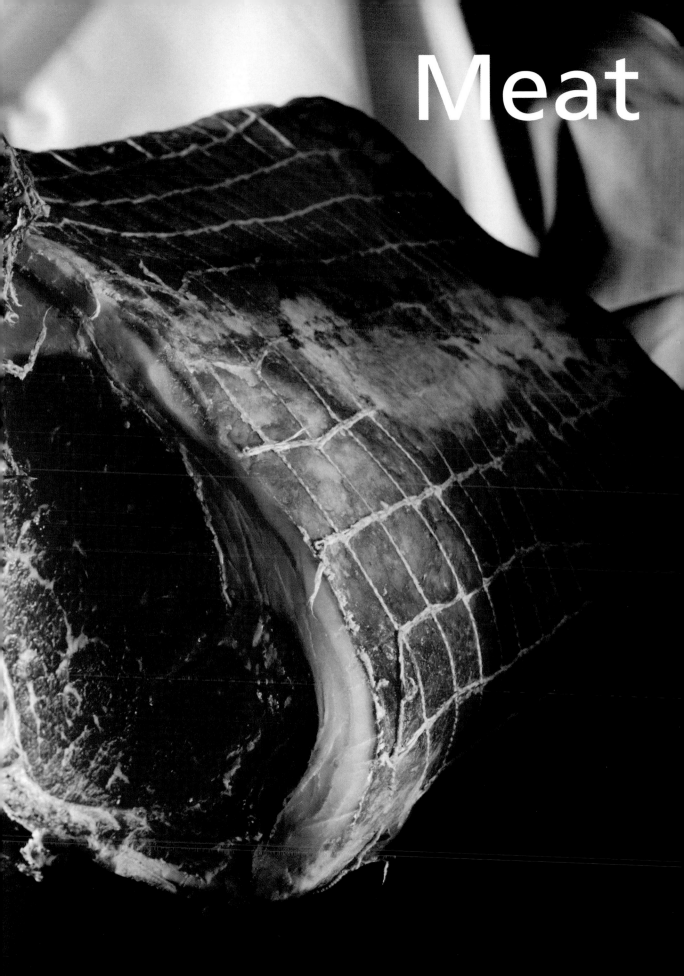

Meat

America is proud of its beef, and rightly so—I love to cook it. Beef here is aged properly so that it is incredibly tender, from juicy skirt steaks to fat marbled rib-eye. I have several meat suppliers and I think it's great that they are still located in the city, most often

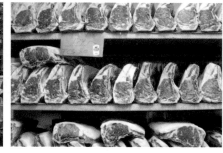

in the meat-packing district. I mostly go to De Bragga and Spitler, to Mark Sarrazin, to d'Artagnan and to Piccinini Brothers. Not only are they all excellent suppliers but they are great people who love what they do and do whatever it takes to get their chefs the best. They constantly search for the best sources of meat and poultry, very important resources for the restaurant world.—DB

“ I'm from Lyons, which I always thought made the best saucisson in the world, but I've discovered Italians can make pretty good ones too. This little Italian corner of the Bronx brings me back to my childhood with the smell of the saucisson and charcuterie. —DB ”

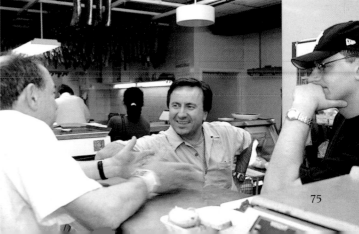

Pork Pate with Pistachios

Makes 1 terrine

- 1 tablespoon extra-virgin olive oil
- 1/4 pound mixed wild mushrooms (such as chanterelles, black trumpets or porcini), trimmed and thinly sliced
- 1/2 shallot, peeled, trimmed and finely chopped
- 2 pounds pork jowls, cut into medium chunks
- 11 ounces pork liver, cut into medium chunks
- 5 ounces chicken livers, cut into medium chunks
- 3 ounces foie gras, cut into medium chunks
- 1/3 cup pistachios, lightly toasted
- 2 tablespoons salt
- 1 teaspoon black peppercorns, finely crushed
- 1/2 teaspoon sel rose
- 1/4 cup all-purpose flour
- 1 large egg, slightly beaten
- 2 tablespoons dry white wine
- 2 tablespoons cognac or brandy
- 5 bay leaves
- 3 sprigs thyme
- 1 tablespoon pink peppercorns

1. Center a rack in the oven and preheat the oven to 350°F.

2. In a medium sauté pan over medium-high heat, warm the olive oil. Add the mushrooms and shallot and cook, stirring occasionally, until tender and any liquid released from the mushrooms has evaporated, about 5 minutes. Set aside to cool and finely chop.

3. Pass the pork jowls, pork and chicken livers and foie gras through a meat grinder set on the medium holes. Transfer the ground meat to the bowl of a mixer fitted with the paddle attachment and add the mushrooms, pistachios, salt, black pepper, sel rose, flour, egg, wine and cognac. Mix together until slightly sticky and pasty.

4. Fill a 4- by 12 1/2-inch terrine mold (1 1/2-quart capacity) with the ground meat, smoothing the top surface with wet fingers. The meat will be about 1/2- to 3/4-inch higher than the sides of the terrine mold. Sprinkle the bay leaves, thyme and pink peppercorns over the forcemeat. Wrap the terrine in aluminum foil and place in a deep baking pan filled with enough water to come halfway up the sides of the mold. Bake in the oven until the internal temperature reads 165°F, on an instant-read thermometer, about 1 1/2 hours.

5. Remove the terrine from the oven and discard the water bath. Let the terrine rest for 10 minutes, then remove the foil. Cover the terrine with a wooden or plastic board and wrap in plastic wrap. Using a 2- to 3-pound weight, such as canned goods, weight the terrine, making sure the weight is distributed evenly; refrigerate for 2 days. The

weight and board can be removed after 1 day or when the terrine is completely cool. Rewrap with plastic wrap. The additional day of refrigeration allows the flavors to meld.

To Serve: Remove the thyme sprigs and bay leaves. Cut and serve the pâté family-style right from the mold. The terrine is served at Café Boulud with mustard vinaigrette, lentils, pickled ramps and baby lettuce.

Wine selection
- Moulin à Vent (France)
  Domaine Louis Jadot-Château
  des Jacques 2000

66 Recently acquired by Louis Jadot, the Château des Jacques produces top-notch Beaujolais. Medium bodied with fresh cherry notes, its acidity absorbs the richness of the pâté well. 99

77

In Chinatown

Borough Hall Farmers Market in Brooklyn

Arthur Avenue in the Bronx

Union Square
Farmers Market

Sweet Aromas

It begins as a lot. It ends up as a little. Crates of vegetables, cases of wine, bushels of bones, bouquets of seasonings and spices. By six o' clock in the morning, bakers, sous chefs and young apprentices begin the transformation of pure product into dinners to die for—or at least, that is the plan. In pans the size of a child's cradle, garlic, leeks, celery root and carrots sizzle and caramelize—sending up thin, hissing clouds of fragrant mist. Lobster shells pan-roasted, deglazed with brandy. Red wine, white wine, infused oils and ancient vinegars glug glugging into huge pots. Buns for the burgers down at db Bistro Moderne, bread for the tables at Café Boulud and Daniel—the smell of baking, sweet and intoxicating. Salsa music in one corner, Led Zeppelin in another, all of it loud. Pans clattering, pastries being brushed. Cauldrons—big enough to poach a small cow—filled with meat and vegetables, wine and bones, gathering the con-centrated essence of ingredients. From now until 5 p.m. a staff of forty-five cooks, bakers and assistants communicate in a cacophonous mixture of French, Japanese, Spanish and English.

(Although they all know the two magic French words in this or any great kitchen, "Oui chef.")

Slowly, because you can't hurry these things, yet swiftly, because it all must be done well before the first patron enters—truckloads, boatloads, planeloads of ingredients marry, blend and meld to become sauces, stocks and half-ready recipes. What started out as twelve bottles of Barolo wine and two gallons of veal stock will come to fit a two-quart saucepan. Soon the work will become more refined, expert, exact. For now, the raw materials for the chefs who will finish and plate the dish are first prepared in this subterranean workroom that is, aptly, as hot as Hades. But the spirit of tonight's meals inhabits these cauldrons and fires. All is possibility and promise and sweet, heady aroma.

Smell is not just a sensory pleasure, it is a very important part of cooking. It is essential to be able to smell, not just taste, each step of food preparation. But restaurants today have very sophisticated fans and vents so that smells dissipate relatively quickly. If you cooked at home the way we do at the restaurant, you would smell it for days! Warm foie gras, highlighted by the sweet smell of roasting apples and toasted hazelnuts; the briny smell of the lobster jus that a cook is preparing for open lobster ravioli with sweet peas; the heady aroma that comes when 10 liters of red wine are reduced to one concentrated cup; the undertones of leeks and carrots being sweated and high notes of herbs, garlic, shallots and roasting meat. Sweet smells of caramel, roasting apricots, warm chocolate and the wonderful smell of freshly baked madeleines floats through the air. —DB

Marinated Pork Shoulder with an Herb Spice Crust

Makes 20 servings

For the Marinade:
- 2 tablespoons coriander seeds
- 1 tablespoon fennel seeds
- 1/2 tablespoon cumin seeds
- 1 tablespoon red pepper flakes
- 1/3 cup honey
- 1 tablespoon Tabasco sauce
- 1/4 cup Worchestershire sauce
- 3 cups unsalted chicken stock or store-bought low-sodium chicken broth
- 3 tablespoons salt
- 1 teaspoon freshly ground pepper
- 10 sprigs thyme
- 1 bunch Italian parsley, leaves and stems separated, leaves reserved for the crust
- 4 bay leaves
- 6 sage leaves, leaves and stems separated, leaves reserved for the crust

In a small sauté pan over low heat, toast the coriander seeds, fennel seeds, cumin seeds and red pepper flakes while constantly stirring until the spices are fragrant, approximately 1 to 2 minutes. Add the honey and continue to cook until it caramelizes to an amber color, approximately 2 to 3 minutes. Deglaze with the Tabasco, Worchestershire sauce and chicken stock. Add the salt, pepper, thyme, parsley stems, bay leaves and sage stems; bring to a boil and cook until the liquid is reduced by one-third, about 20 minutes. Let the marinade cool and strain through a fine-mesh sieve.

For the Herb Spice Crust:
- Reserved parsley leaves, finely chopped
- Reserved sage leaves, finely chopped
- 1 tablespoon ground coriander
- 1 1/2 teaspoons ground cumin
- 1 tablespoon coarsely ground black pepper
- 1 tablespoon ground fennel
- 1/4 cup extra-virgin olive oil

> **"** I love pork, but it needs fat to taste great; so, after bacon, the shoulder is my favorite cut. This recipe was prepared by Michael David, the sous-chef at db Bistro, for the staff there. It isn't quite barbecue, it isn't quite braised; it's rubbed with a lot of spices and cooked very slowly. You have to baste it often so the spices melt into the meat. It's not spicy hot but very flavorful. I call it "Burgundy meets Memphis." It's perfect for when you have lots of friends coming over and you want to be able to spend time with them—you start it Saturday night for lunch on Sunday. It's perfect served simply with baked potatoes and a green salad. **"**
> —DB

In a small bowl, combine all the ingredients.

For the Pork Shoulder:
- One 12-pound bone-in pork shoulder

1. Preheat the oven to 500°F.
2. Score the pork shoulder skin in a diamond pattern, making the lines 3/4-inch apart. Inject the Marinade into the shoulder using a hypodermic needle or baster-injector. Rub the spice mixture into the skin of the pork. Place the shoulder in a large roasting

pan, slide the pan into the oven and roast for 20 minutes. Reduce the heat to 200°F, place a baking pan of hot water on the lowest rack of the oven and continue to roast until the outside is dark, crusty and golden brown and the meat is falling off the bones, 10 to 12 hours. Remove the shoulder from the oven and let rest approximately 1 hour before serving.

To Serve: Carefully transfer the shoulder to a large platter and serve family-style.

Wine selection
- Russian River Valley Zinfandel, California (U.S.)
  Hendry "Block #7" 1999

66 This flavorful, slow-cooked preparation is tender enough to warrant a rich and tannic wine with spicy aromatic notes, such as this delicious Zinfandel from Napa Valley. 99

Guinea Hen Terrine

Makes 1 terrine

- 1 pound boneless guinea hen meat (breast or leg) from a 2 1/2 pound bird
- 12 ounces fresh pork belly
- 5 ounces fresh foie gras, denerved and deveined
- 4 ounces chicken livers
- 1 tablespoon finely chopped garlic
- 2 tablespoons dry white wine
- 1 tablespoon cognac or brandy
- 1 sprig thyme, leaves only, chopped
- 1 tablespoon plus 1 teaspoon sel rose
- 1 teaspoon freshly ground white pepper
- 1/4 teaspoon four-spice (equal amounts of freshly ground black pepper, ground cinnamon, ground nutmeg and ground cloves)
- 3 ounces country bacon
- 3 ounces smoked bacon

1. Cut the guinea hen meat into strips. In a large bowl, combine the hen with the pork belly, foie gras, chicken livers, garlic, white wine, brandy, thyme, sel rose, pepper and four-spice. Cover with plastic wrap, and let the meats marinate overnight in the refrigerator.

2. Center a rack in the oven and preheat the oven to 250°F.

3. Pass the meat mixture and bacons through a meat grinder set on the medium holes. Transfer the ground meat to the bowl of a mixer fitted with the paddle attachment. Mix together until slightly sticky and pasty.

4. Fill a 4- by 12 1/2-inch terrine mold (1 1/2-quart capacity) with the ground meat, smoothing the top surface with wet fingers. Wrap the terrine mold in aluminum foil and place in a deep baking pan filled with enough water to come halfway up the mold. Bake until the internal temperature reads 165°F on an instant-read thermometer, about 1 1/2 to 2 hours. Remove the terrine from the oven and discard the water bath.

5. Let the terrine rest for 10 minutes, then remove the foil. Cover the terrine with a wooden or plastic board and wrap in plastic wrap. Using a 2- to 3-pound weight or canned goods, weight the terrine, making sure the weight is distributed evenly. Refrigerate for 24 hours. Remove the weight and board when the terrine is completely cool. Use a wet towel to remove any excess fat from the outside of the terrine. Rewrap with clean plastic wrap. Refrigerate for another 24 hours before serving to allow the flavors to meld evenly.

To Serve:
Cut and serve the pâté family-style right from the mold with slices of warm toasted sourdough bread lightly rubbed with a garlic clove. At db Bistro we serve this dish with pickled turnips, pickled baby shiitakes, pickled ginger and pickled ramps.

Wine selection
- Rheingau Riesling (Germany)
  Robert Weil-Kabinett
  Halbtrocken 2000

66 Light and dry and with a lively acidity, this nicely balanced Riesling from Germany shines through the smooth grain of this richly flavored terrine. 99

66 I like to play around with the traditional idea of pickling. I love to pickle fruit, cherries, grapes, rhubarb. It's always important to have some sugar in the vinegar—to play with the sweet and sour, the saltiness and spiciness. Pickles are an important element of charcuterie because they cut the fat—all of our pickling is geared to serve with pate, terrine, saucisson and strong meat and game. There's a lot of creativity in condiments, and pickles are a type that play a small but very key role in a dish. —DB 99

Chicken Provencal

Makes 4 servings

- One 3- to 4-pound chicken
- 1/2 cup extra-virgin olive oil
- Salt and freshly ground pepper
- 2 tablespoons all-purpose flour
- 8 spring onions, white part with 1/2-inch of green only
- 1 red pepper, split, seeded and cut into 1/2-inch thick strips
- 8 small Yukon Gold or 16 Fingerling potatoes, peeled
- 1 cup dry white wine
- 3 cups unsalted chicken stock or store-bought low-sodium chicken broth
- 1 tablespoon tomato paste
- 4 large tomatoes, peeled, seeded and cut into 2-inch chunks
- 3 cloves garlic, peeled
- 1 bay leaf
- 1 sprig thyme
- 3 ounces haricot verts, tipped
- 1 cup fava beans, shelled (about 1 pound in pod)
- 1 medium eggplant, washed, trimmed and cut into 1-inch chunks
- 1 medium zucchini, washed, trimmed and cut into 1-inch chunks
- 1/3 cup black olives, pitted

1. Cut the chicken into 8 parts. First, cut off the legs. Then cut each leg in two, separating the thigh from the drumstick. Next, using poultry shears, detach the backbone all the way to the neck; chop both the backbone and neck into 2 to 3 pieces. Split the pair of breasts down the center and then split each breast crosswise in half.

2. Warm 1/4 cup of the olive oil in a Dutch oven or large casserole over medium-high heat. Season the chicken all over with salt and pepper and dust with the flour. When the oil is hot, slip the chicken into the pot and sear on all sides until well browned, about 10 minutes. Add the onions, red pepper and potatoes and stir until the vegetables are coated with oil. Deglaze with the wine and reduce by half. Add the stock, tomato paste, tomatoes, garlic, bay leaf and thyme and season with salt and pepper. Bring the liquid to a boil over high heat, reduce the heat to medium and simmer for 30 minutes.

3. Bring a large pot of salted water to a boil. Prepare an ice-water bath in a small bowl. Plunge the haricot verts into the boiling water and blanch for approximately 5 minutes. Immediately put the fava beans in a colander and plunge the colander into the pot so that the beans are submerged and can boil for 3 minutes. Remove the colander with the fava beans. With a slotted spoon or tongs, transfer the haricot verts to the prepared ice-water bath. Hold the fava beans under cold running water to cool them. When cool, drain the haricot verts well and pop the fava beans out of their shells. Rinse the peeled fava beans under cold water and pat dry. Set the beans and haricot verts aside until needed.

4. Warm the remaining 1/4 cup olive oil in a large sauté pan over medium-high heat. Add the eggplant and zucchini and cook until golden brown, approximately 8 minutes. Transfer the eggplant and zucchini to a plate lined with paper towels to drain.

5. Add the haricot verts, fava beans, eggplant and zucchini to the chicken and cook it all together for an additional 10 minutes. Stir in the olives and season with salt and pepper, if needed. Discard the bay leaf and thyme. Serve family-style rightfrom the pot.

Wine selection
- Bandol (France) Château de Pibarnon 1998

❝ Medium bodied with dark fruit and Provençal herb overtones, this Mourvèdre-based wine is complex yet rustic enough so as not to overshadow the mixed flavors of the vegetables and herbs, yet stand up to the preparation of the chicken. ❞

" This is quintessential "cuisine bourgeoise." It's simple, a bit rustic and definitely homey. It's a one-pot dish with many depths of flavor that blend together into a taste of Provence. I would put this dish on the menu as a special with as much pride as I would serve it at home on Sunday. —DB. **"**

Pozole

Makes 30 servings

At the café, we make this soup the traditional way, with a pig's head. But you can also make it with pork shoulder or chicken. If you have access to a pig's head, ask your butcher to remove the eyes and then degorge the head in water for 2 days. Every time we make this staff-meal, the ingredients change depending on what's available in the restaurant. Please feel free to be creative with the side dishes.

- Two 4-pound chickens, one 8-pound pork shoulder or one 10-pound pig's head
- 3 gallons water
- 4 onions, peeled and roughly chopped
- 1/2 stalk celery
- 5 bay leaves
- One 6-pound can precooked hominy, rinsed and drained
- 1/4 cup dried Mexican oregano or regular dried oregano
- Salt
- 2 packages fried tortilla or nachos
- 2 cups tomatoes, cut into 1/4-inch dice
- 2 heads romaine lettuce, outer leaves removed, cut into very thin strips
- 2 cups red onions or shallots, cut into 1/4-inch dice
- 2 cups radish, cut into 1/4-inch dice
- 1 cup jalapeño peppers, cut into 1/4-inch dice
- 1 cup cilantro leaves
- 10 limes, cut into wedges

1. In a large stockpot, bring the chicken (or pork shoulder or pig's head), water, onions, celery and bay leaves to a boil. Reduce the heat to a simmer and cook the meat until tender, 3 to 4 hours, while skimming and removing any froth and scum from the broth. Remove the meat and let cool. If you are using chicken or a pig's head, shred the meat. If using pork, cut the meat into small pieces. Strain the broth through a fine-mesh sieve.

2. Add half of the strained broth to the meat. Bring the other half to a low simmer, add the hominy and cook for 5 minutes. Add the oregano and the meat with the reserved broth and cook until everything is heated through. Season with salt, if necessary.

Serve the tomatoes, lettuce, onions, radish, jalapeño peppers, cilantro and limes on the side to be added to the soup or served with the fried tortillas.

Wine selection
- Mexican Beer
  Corona or Pacifico

serve Family-style right from the pot

Lunch
Midtown/Uptown

"Gimme a hot dog with mustard and kraut."
"Gimme a slice with pepperoni and peppers."
"What do ya got that's fast?"
"C'mon, the light's changing!"

At lunch time for most of New York, eating is an exercise in speed. How fast can you order, pay for, gobble up a meal and get back to your desk, your class, your gym, your shrink, your . . . whatever. Where Paris is devoted to style, New York is devoted to speed. The leisurely lunch combines two words that have no meaning in Manhattan.

Midtown: concrete, glass and steel with people wedged in like mortar in brick work. The streets are as crammed as the Tokyo subway. The traffic signals are frozen in a permanent "Don't Walk" that is universally ignored. Somehow the street vendors, a largely Senegalese fraternity, manage to find space to hawk their Chanel and Rolex knockoffs and authentic-ish African artifacts manufactured last week in a loft in Queens.

Take all this Manhattan activity, compress it, speed it up by two and surround it by flashing neon lights and video screens displaying

12:00 p.m.

young bodies—sipping soft drinks, filling up skin-tight jeans and T-shirts, setting global standards of thinness and good looks—that are the envy and desire of the overheated, overscheduled lunch-hour multitudes below. Times Square.

For years, the answer to the question, "Where can I find a good meal in the theater district?" was, "Leave the theater district." It was a tired old neighborhood with tired old French and Italian joints that offered tableside nostalgia (all those perkily signed pictures of Frank Sinatra, Richard Burton and well coiffed and forgettable soap opera stars) and a menu as old and beaten up as the pictures. Or, more recently, souped- up theme park restaurants—the theme park being "New Yorkland," a fantasized, sanitized, pimp-less, hooker-less, crime-free Times Square with assembly-line food endorsed by super-models, basketball stars and other celebs who have nothing to do with dining. Guaranteed to get you out in time for the show.

In the midst of this, next door to the Algonquin, where Hemingway and Parker, Benchley and Ferber met daily for lunch, there is db Bistro Moderne—presided over by a young chef, Jean-François Bruel, who, like Daniel, is straight out of Lyon and the three-star kitchens of southern France. It's a modern Parisian bistro—in other words, it doesn't have faux layers of paint on the walls turned faux yellow from faux cigarette smoke with faux Cynar posters hanging above faux antiqued leather banquettes.

db Bistro Moderne could just as well be somewhere on rue Segur, a place where a young chef could serve simple fare and a few modern experiments. Chic, not retro. And the most over-the-top hamburger recipe (foie gras and pulled shortribs swaddled in sirloin) since the domestication of cattle in 6000 B.C.

db Bistro Moderne is a *bon chic bon genre* restaurant in midtown Manhattan. It's a bit French, a bit Parisian, and quite American. The body and soul of the uptown restaurant remains, only the exterior changes.. I wanted red, not all red, but a bit of red, like the way you used to see red banquettes in Parisian brasseries, very classic. The front of the house more like a cafe, the back more like a restaurant. Women definitely look gorgeous against those mustard gold walls . . .We made the decision that we were going to be a bistro, a great bistro. db is just taking Daniel out of his suit and putting him in blue jeans.

"d

Jean-François has a lot of qualities that remind me of myself when I was his age. My friend, André Barcet, a chef in Saint Etienne, recommended Jean-François to me and asked me to take good care of him. Jean-François comes from a small town about forty miles south of Lyon. He spent some time at three-Michelin-starred Haeberlin and then came to Daniel and worked for me for three years. After that, he went to Michel Guérard in France, where I also once worked. Then back to New York as sous chef at Café Boulud and now he is the chef at db.

b"

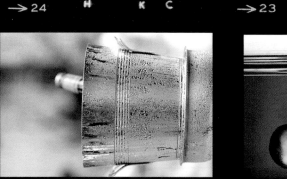

Café
Boulud

The Melting Pot

Take the Number 7 train from Grand Central Station out to Queens. Along the way you will pass through communities of Greeks, Koreans, Italians, Chinese, Bengalis, Irish, Pakistanis, Mexicans, Uruguayans, Spaniards, Dominicans, Russians, Poles, Malays—there is a little bit of every nation in New York. In fact, more than a little bit—and that is the key to the culinary diversity and vigor of the city's dining heritage.

There is a pizza shop on every block that, were it in the hinterlands, would attract diners from fifty miles around. The hot dogs, sauerkraut and soggy steamed buns of the sidewalk vendors and the falafel, roast chestnuts, sausage and peppers of street corner carts fill the avenues of every borough with aromas of meat, onions and spices.

Food is never more than a step away—interesting food at that. There are more Italians in New York than in Rome, more Irish than in Dublin, more Jews than in Jerusalem. The sheer size of New York's ethnic communities means that the food is authentic: One Bengali family in a town isn't going to affect the supermarkets, but ten thousand families will be able to support farms, importers, chefs. New York's ethnic groups have reached gastronomic critical mass.

Add to that mix a population that considers restaurant dining to be one of the supreme urban pleasures and you begin to understand why and how this international spirit has energized even the most classique haute cuisine restaurants.

Daniel's work force includes French, Chinese, Japanese, Mexican, Senegalese, Korean, Bengali, Ecuadorian, Bosnian, Czech, Austrian, Puerto Rican, Italian. Though the theme, the organizing principle of their work, is French (in the same way that air traffic control, no matter what country, is conducted in English), there is an international sensibility that has infused all three of Daniel's restaurants; indeed, it's infused all New York restaurants.

This is just the local version of a global trend that combines French culinary technique with international style. Café Boulud is dedicated to exploring global cuisine while celebrating the home cooking of Daniel's heritage in St. Pierre. Each month Andrew Carmellini—a young, intensively schooled chef—and Daniel create a new menu inspired by a different national cuisine. To that they add a menu based on the season, a vegetarian menu and traditional *cuisine bourgeoise*.

At Café Boulud, different, constantly different is the raison d'être. If the goal at Daniel is simple perfection, the goal at Café Boulud is the perfectly delicious surprise.

Sugar Cane Grilled Shrimp with Peanut Sauce

Makes 4 to 6 appetizer servings

For the Spicy Peanut Sauce (makes 1 cup):
- 1/2 teaspoon crushed red pepper flakes
- 1/2 cup peanut oil
- 1/2 stalk lemongrass, ends trimmed, tough outer leaves removed and tender heart of bulb thinly sliced
- One 1/2-inch piece peeled ginger, thinly sliced
- 3 tablespoons rice wine vinegar
- 2 tablespoons sugar
- 2 teaspoons Asian fish sauce (preferably nuoc nam)
- 1 clove garlic, peeled and sliced
- 1 kaffir lime leaf
- 3/4 cup salted, roasted peanuts
- 1/4 cup water

1. In a medium sauté pan, toast the red pepper flakes over medium-high heat until dry and fragrant, about 2 minutes. Add the peanut oil, lemongrass and ginger and cook for 5 minutes. Add the vinegar, sugar and fish sauce, reduce the heat to low and simmer for 2 minutes. Add the garlic, kaffir lime leaf and all but 2 tablespoons of the peanuts and simmer for 5 minutes more. Remove the lime leaf.

2. Transfer the mixture to a blender or food processor and purée until smooth. Gradually add the water and purée until a creamy consistency is reached. Add additional water, if needed. Chop the remaining 2 tablespoons of peanuts. Transfer the sauce to a serving bowl and garnish with the chopped peanuts.

For the Shrimp Marinade:
- One 12-inch piece fresh sugar cane, (or 15 large toothpicks, 3 inches long)
- 1/2 cup extra-virgin olive oil
- 1/2 stalk lemongrass, tough outer leaves removed, crushed
- One 1/2-inch piece ginger, peeled and thinly sliced
- 1 clove garlic, peeled and sliced
- 2 sprigs mint, leaves only
- 1 pound jumbo shrimp (about 15) peeled, deveined and tails removed
- Salt and freshly ground pepper

1. Using a large chef's knife or cleaver, cut two 4- to 6-inch-long sticks from the center of the sugar cane. Stand the sticks on end. Using a serrated knife, carefully cut straight down on four sides of the cylinder, peeling away the outer layer of skin, forming a rectangle. Cut the rectangle lengthwise into 3 slices, about 1/4-inch thick. Cut each slice into 3 skewers. Trim one end to a v-shaped point. Repeat the process until you have one skewer per shrimp; set aside.

2. In a small bowl, whisk together the oil, lemongrass, ginger, garlic and mint leaves. Skewer each shrimp and place in a container large enough to hold the shrimp in a single layer. Pour the marinade over the shrimp; cover and refrigerate at least 8 hours or overnight.

3. Place a grill pan over medium-high heat. Remove the shrimp from the marinade and cook for 1 1/2 to 2 minutes per side. Season with salt and pepper.

Serve with the peanut sauce.

Our own cocktail, the "Mojó 65"
- 1/2 Marti Rum
- 1/4 Fresh Grapefruit juice
- 1/4 Tonic Water
- Garnish with lime and mint leaf

To enjoy on the patio on a hot summer night; a fusion of the Far East and the Caribbean. Sip on this refreshing drink, fruity with a nice send-off from the lime and mint.

Salted Cod Fritters

Makes 75 hors d'oeuvres

- 2 pounds salt cod
- 20 cloves garlic, peeled and crushed
- 2 quarts whole milk
- 1 herb sachet (5 sprigs thyme, 2 sprigs rosemary, 2 tablespoons whole black peppercorns, 2 tablespoons coriander seeds, 1 bay cheesecloth)
- 2 tablespoons extra-virgin olive oil
- 1/2 red bell pepper, core and seeds removed and cut into 1/8-inch dice
- 1/2 yellow bell pepper, core and seeds removed and cut into 1/8-inch dice
- 1 California carrot, trimmed, peeled and cut into 1/8-inch dice
- 2 small stalks celery, trimmed, peeled and cut into 1/8-inch dice
- 1 teaspoon piment d'espellette
- Salt and freshly ground pepper
- 1 1/2 cups all-purpose flour
- 4 large eggs
- 1 tablespoon finely chopped tarragon
- 1 tablespoon finely chopped chives
- 1 tablespoon finely chopped Italian parsley leaves
- 1 tablespoon finely chopped chervil leaves
- Peanut oil, for deep frying
- 3/4 cup fresh bread crumbs

1. The day before you make the fritters, trim the salt cod, cutting away all the dry parts around the belly and tail. Once trimmed, you should have about 1 1/2 pounds of perfectly white cod fillet. Cut the fillet into 2- to 3-inch chunks, put the pieces in a Dutch oven or stockpot and cover the fish with cold water. Keep the fish submerged in the cold water and refrigerate for 24 hours, changing the water three to four times during this period.

Wine selection
- Ribeiro (Spain)
  Viña Mein 1999

66 Citronella and orange rind aromas dominate this lively Spanish white wine assertive enough for the cod fritters but light enough for a cocktail party. 99

2. In a small pot, bring the cod, garlic, milk and herb sachet to a simmer and slowly poach the fish until tender and fully cooked, about 30 minutes. Gently remove the cod from the pot using a slotted fish spatula or 2 pancake spatulas and set aside. Strain the poaching liquid through a fine-mesh sieve; reserve 2 cups of the poaching liquid.

3. Warm the olive oil in a large sauté pan over medium-high heat. Add the bell peppers, carrot and celery and cook, while stirring, until the vegetables are tender but have no color, 10 to 15 minutes. Season with piment d'espellette, salt and pepper. Let the vegetables cool.

4. Beat together 1 cup of the flour and 2 of the eggs. In a large bowl using a wooden spoon, stir the cod until it is slightly crushed. Add the vegetables, the flour-egg mixture, the herbs and the reserved poaching liquid. Mix until all the ingredients are incorporated. Take care not to overmix: You want the mixture to be well crushed, but still coarse and even a bit lumpy. The mixture should mound and hold its shape on a spoon, like mashed potatoes.

5. Pour 3 to 4 inches of peanut oil into a deep pot or casserole and heat the oil to 325°F, as measured by a deep-fat thermometer.

6. Using a spoon or a small ice cream scoop, form small balls 3/4-inch to 1-inch in diameter. Lightly beat the remaining 2 eggs. Dip each fritter first into the remaining 1/2 cup flour, then the eggs and finally the bread crumbs, making sure to coat them evenly. Gently tap off any excess. Fry the fritters in batches until golden brown, 2 to 3 minutes for each batch. Carefully lift the fritters out of the oil and onto a plate lined with a double thickness of paper towels. Pat off any excess oil and season with salt and pepper. Serve immediately.

Cod, garlic, milk, herb sachet, piment d'Espelette

Butternut Squash Soup with Exotic Spices, Apples & Cilantro Cream

Makes 12 appetizer servings

For the Soup:
- 2 small butternut squash (1 3/4 pounds each)
- 2 tablespoons unsalted butter
- 1 large onion, peeled and thinly sliced
- 1 tablespoon Madras curry powder
- One 1-inch piece fresh ginger, peeled and sliced
- 1 clove garlic, peeled and sliced
- Salt and freshly ground pepper
- 1 cup unsweetened coconut milk
- 5 cups unsalted chicken stock or store-bought low-sodium chicken broth

1. Trim the ends of each squash. Cut each squash crosswise into 3 wheels. Using a vegetable peeler, remove the skin. Cut each wheel in half and use a spoon to remove the seeds. Cut the squash into 1/2-inch cubes and set aside.

2. In a large stockpot or casserole, melt the butter over medium heat. Add the onion and cook, stirring, until it is tender but does not color, about 10 minutes. Add the curry powder, ginger and garlic and cook for 2 minutes. Add the squash, season with salt and pepper, and sauté for 1 minute. Stir in the coconut milk and chicken stock, bring to a boil and then reduce to a simmer. Cook, stirring occasionally, until the squash is tender when pierced with a fork, about 20 minutes.

Wine selection
- Alsace Gewurztraminer (France) "Altenbourg" Domaine Paul Blanck 2000

66I love the interaction between the richness of this wine with linden aromas and the unctuousness of the spiced soup.**99**

3. Using a blender or food processor purée the soup, working in batches, until smooth. Strain through a fine-mesh sieve and season with salt and pepper, if needed. (The soup can be cooled completely and stored in a covered container in the refrigerator for up to two days. Bring the soup to a boil before serving.)

For the Apple Compote (makes 3/4 cup) :
- 3/4 teaspoon coriander seeds
- 1/4 teaspoon ground cumin
- 2 tablespoons unsalted butter
- 2 Granny Smith apples, peeled, cored and roughly chopped
- 1/2 cup apple cider
- 1 teaspoon kocum, seeded and diced (dried Indian fruit)

1. In a small sauté pan over medium heat, separately toast the coriander seeds and cumin powder, swirling the pan, until fragrant, about 3 to 5 minutes. Finely grind them in a spice grinder.

2. Cook the butter in a small saucepan over high heat until light golden brown. Add the apples and cook, stirring, until caramelized, about 5 minutes. Add the apple cider and cook until the liquid has evaporated, about 6 to 8 minutes. Transfer the apples to a blender or food processor and purée until smooth. (The compote should be thick.) Mix in the coriander-cumin spice mixture and kocum, set aside and keep warm.

For the Cilantro Cream:
- 1/2 cup heavy cream
- 1 teaspoon finely chopped cilantro leaves
- Salt and freshly ground pepper

Whip the heavy cream, cilantro, salt and pepper until stiff peaks form. Refrigerate until ready to use.

To Serve:
- 1 teaspoon dana dal (toasted inside of a coriander seed)
- Cilantro sprigs

Reheat the soup, if necessary. Place a tablespoon of the apple compote into the center of each warm soup bowl. Carefully ladle the soup into the bowl. Sprinkle the soup with the dana dal. Place 1 heaping tablespoon of the cilantro cream in each bowl. Garnish with the cilantro sprigs.

Café Boulud

"Daniel is my ultimate French gastronomic restaurant—I want Café Boulud to be French-American. What does that mean? It means half of it has the soul and spirit of France and myself, and the other half has the cuisines of the whole world, of the "American melting pot."

If I were thirty years old and starting out, I'd be much more global than French. So when I created Café Boulud I wanted to make sure that I encouraged the chefs to keep open minds and to explore things that we, or I, didn't dare do until now, like Middle Eastern or Chinese or Mexican cuisines. Andrew, the chef, and I discussed the various dishes he likes to cook, and we involved the other cooks as well, drawing on their backgrounds and knowledge.

For example, pozole, which is often on the Mexican menu at Café Boulud, was started by a Mexican prep cook who made it for the staff meal. They all liked it so much that Andrew talked to me about putting it on the menu.

So, you see, we have no problem asking Pedro what his mother cooks."

—DB

110

Andrew Carmellini

" Andrew has a very rounded training, and Café Boulud has been a great opportunity for him to express several different styles of cuisine. He came out of a pivotal New York restaurant, Lespinasse, and learned from Gray Kunz. He worked at San Dominico, where he drew upon his Italian heritage—I'm a big fan of his delicate and unique pastas and gnocchi. Then he went to Le Cirque, and his time there helped him understand more about the New York restaurant business and how one of New York's classic restaurants operates.

Andrew is the quintessential American-European chef because he has a great understanding of French and Italian cuisine, to which he brings a very personal American touch. He's very talented and I appreciate that he still wants to learn. He's constantly motivated by his vision and passion for cooking.

I love exploring little neighborhoods with Andrew; it's always a lot of fun. He's discreet. He's modest. He's good, he's careful. He's wise, but also he's a fun guy. —DB "

Roasted Beet and Endive Salad with Chevre & Pistachio Vinaigrette

Makes 4 appetizer servings

For the Pistachio Vinaigrette:
- 1 tablespoon unsweetened pistachio paste or 1/4 cup pistachios puréed in a food processor to a smooth paste
- 1 1/2 tablespoons pistachio oil
- 1 1/2 tablespoons grapeseed oil
- 1 tablespoon sherry vinegar
- Salt and freshly ground pepper
- 2 tablespoons water

In a bowl, using a whisk or hand-held immersion blender, whisk the pistachio paste, oils and vinegar until smooth. Stir in enough water to thin the vinaigrette to a pouring consistency. Season with salt and pepper.

For the Beet Rosace:
- 1 large red beet, scrubbed
- 1 large yellow beet, scrubbed
- Pistachio Vinaigrette (from recipe above)
- Salt and freshly ground pepper

1. Center a rack in the oven and preheat the oven to 400°F.
2. Wrap each beet individually in aluminum foil. Place the beets on a sheet pan and bake until the beets are easily pierced with a fork or knife, about 1 hour. Let the beets cool enough to handle. Wearing plastic gloves to prevent staining your hands, use a small paring knife to remove the skins.
3. Using a chef's knife or mandoline, slice the beets paper thin (about 1/16-inch thick). Using a 2-inch round cutter, cut one circle out of each slice. Coarsely chop the red and yellow beet scraps separately and reserve for the tartar.

4. Lay an 8-inch square piece of plastic wrap on a flat surface. Arrange 6 beet slices in a 4 1/2-inch circle, slightly overlapping the slices, leaving a small hole in the center. Season with salt and pepper, drizzle 1 teaspoon Pistachio Vinaigrette on top and cover with a second 8-inch square piece of plastic wrap. Repeat with the remaining beet slices, forming three more beet rosaces; refrigerate until needed.

For the Beet Tartar:
- Reserved beet scraps, about 2 cups
- 3 tablespoons extra-virgin olive oil
- 1 tablespoon sherry vinegar
- Salt and freshly ground pepper

Place all of the ingredients in a bowl and gently mix together. Season with salt and pepper. Refrigerate until needed.

For the Beet Reduction:
- 1/2 cup homemade or store-bought beet juice

In a small sauté pan, bring the beet juice to a low simmer and reduce by three-quarters, about 8 minutes. If using homemade juice, strain through a fine-mesh sieve. Keep at room temperature until needed.

For the Goat Cheese Balls:
- 2 ounces goat cheese, softened
- 1 teaspoon heavy cream
- 1 teaspoon sherry vinegar
- 1 tablespoon finely chopped shallots
- 1 tablespoon finely chopped chives
- 2 sprigs thyme, leaves only
- Salt and freshly ground pepper
- 1 1/2 ounces roasted unsalted pistachios, finely chopped

1. In a small bowl, mix together the goat cheese, cream, vinegar, shallots, chives and thyme. Season with salt and pepper. Chill in refrigerator for 15 minutes.
2. Divide the cheese mixture into fourths and form four balls. Roll each ball in the chopped pistachio nuts to coat. Reserve any unused nuts. Refrigerate the goat cheese balls until needed.

To Assemble and Serve:

1. Preheat the oven to 300°F. Place the Goat Cheese Balls on a parchment paper-lined baking sheet. Heat until just warmed through, about 5 minutes.

2. Fill a 2 1/2- by 1-inch-high ring three-quarters full with the Beet Tartar. Using the back of a spoon, press down on the beets until they fill the ring halfway. Fill the ring with some of the Frisée and Endive Salad and place a warm goat cheese ball on top of the salad. Carefully lift and remove the ring. Repeat with remaining rings. Set aside the remaining Frisée and Endive Salad.

3. Remove the Beet Rosaces from the refrigerator. Gently peel off and discard the top layers of plastic wrap. Carefully invert one rosace on top of each Goat Cheese Ball, leaving it beet side down. Peel off the remaining plastic wrap.

4. Spoon some of the pistachio vinaigrette around each beet crown, drizzle the beet reduction over the vinaigrette, and sprinkle the remaining pistachio nuts around the plate. Stick three endive spears into the center of each beet circle (there should be a hole).

For the Frisée and Endive Salad:

- 1 small Belgian endive
- 3 tablespoons extra-virgin olive oil
- 1 tablespoon sherry vinegar
- 1 medium head frisée, white and yellow parts only, trimmed, washed, dried and cut into 1-inch long pieces
- Salt and freshly ground pepper

1. Remove four endive leaves. Cut each leaf lengthwise into thirds or spears. Wrap in damp paper towels and refrigerate until ready to serve.

2. Cut each endive core crosswise into thin slices. In a small bowl whisk together the olive oil and vinegar. Mix in the sliced endive and frisée and season with salt and pepper.

Place small mound salad between endive spears hold them up serve immediately.

Wine selection
- Touraine Sauvignon Blanc (France)
  Clos Roche Blanche 2000

" Produced organically, this wine is very dry and mineral with some zesty aromatic notes. It makes for a playful companion to the sweetness of the beets and the bitterness of the endives. "

Tomato Tart Tatin

Makes 8 appetizer servings

For the Pistou Sauce (makes 1 cup):

The pistou can be made one day ahead of time and kept covered in the refrigerator. Bring to room temperature and stir before using. Extra sauce can be tossed with pasta or spread on toasted croutons or sandwiches. Store in an airtight container, refrigerated, up to 1 week or freeze up to 1 month.

- 2 bunches basil (about 8 ounces), leaves only
- 1/2 clove garlic, peeled; reserve remaining half for Herb Goat Cheese
- 1 teaspoon pine nuts, lightly toasted
- 1 teaspoon grated Parmesan cheese
- 1/2 cup extra-virgin olive oil

1. Bring a medium pot of salted water to a boil. Plunge the basil into the boiling water and blanch for 2 minutes. Drain the leaves and hold under cold running water to stop the cooking process. Drain and squeeze the leaves of excess water.
2. Put all the ingredients in the bowl of a food processor fitted with the steel blade attachment. Process until smooth, about 2 minutes. Transfer to an airtight container and refrigerate.

For the Puff Pastry:

- 1 pound frozen puff pastry
- Egg wash: 1 egg whisked with 1 teaspoon water

1. Center a rack in the oven and preheat the oven to 400°F.
2. On a lightly floured surface with a floured rolling pin, roll the puff pastry to a 3/16-inch thickness. Using a 4-inch round cutter, cut the dough into 8 discs. Place the discs on a parchment paper-lined baking sheet and refrigerate for 15 minutes. Brush the discs with the egg wash. Dock the dough by pricking the surface with a fork. Bake until golden brown, 10 to 12 minutes. Transfer to a wire rack to cool.

For the Tomatoes:

- 10 large plum tomatoes, cut crosswise into 1/8-inch thick slices
- Salt and freshly ground pepper
- 2 tablespoons extra-virgin olive oil

1. To remove excess moisture from the tomato slices, place them in an even layer on baking sheets lined with several layers of paper or kitchen towels. Season with salt. Allow the slices to drain in the refrigerator for 2 to 3 hours.
2. Center a rack in the oven and preheat the oven to 350°F.
3. Brush the bottoms of eight 4-inch nonstick round tart molds with the olive oil. Arrange the tomato slices in an overlapping circle, about 12 per pan. Season with salt and pepper. Place the pans onto a baking sheet and bake until the tomatoes are soft, about 10 minutes. Using the back of a spoon, press the tomatoes flat. Set aside until needed.

For the Caramelized Onions:

- 2 tablespoons unsalted butter
- 2 medium yellow onions (about 7 ounces each), peeled and thinly sliced
- 4 sprigs thyme, leaves only
- Salt and freshly ground pepper

In a large sauté pan, melt the butter over medium-low heat. Add the onions and thyme and season with salt and pepper. Cook, stirring, until the onions start to caramelize, 12 to 15 minutes. When brown, remove and set aside until needed.

For the Herb Goat Cheese:

- 4 ounces fresh goat cheese, softened
- 2 teaspoons mascarpone cheese
- 2 teaspoons heavy cream
- 2 tablespoons Pistou Sauce (from recipe above)
- 2 tablespoons finely chopped shallots
- 2 tablespoons finely chopped chives
- 1 teaspoon finely chopped garlic
- Salt and freshly ground pepper

In a small bowl, mix together the cheeses, cream, Pistou Sauce, shallots, chives and garlic. Season with salt and pepper. Set aside until needed.

For the Frisée Salad:

- 2 small heads frisée, white and light yellow parts only, trimmed
- 8 small white mushrooms, thinly sliced
- 1/2 cup kalamata olives (about 16), pitted and halved
- 16 cherry tomatoes, cut in half
- 2 tablespoons chervil leaves
- 8 chives, cut into 1/2-inch pieces
- 1/4 cup extra-virgin olive oil
- 1 tablespoon freshly squeezed lemon juice
- Salt and freshly ground pepper

In a medium bowl, toss together the frisée, mushrooms, olives, tomatoes, chervil, chives, olive oil and lemon juice. Season with salt and pepper.

To Serve:

Divide the herb goat cheese evenly among the 8 molds, placing a scoop in the center of the warm tomatoes. Divide the warm caramelized onions evenly over the goat cheese and top with a puff pastry circle. Invert each mold onto the center of a plate and remove the molds. If necessary, use a spoon and gently tap the bottom of the molds to release the tatins. Place a small mound of the frisée salad on top. Drizzle the pistou sauce around the plate

Wine selection
- Côteaux du Languedoc (France) Domaine les Aurelles-Aurel 1998

66 The acidity of the tomatoes and texture of the cheese work well with this rich, low-acid blend of Roussane and Marsanne from the south of France. 99

115

Boeuf en Gelee

Makes 6 to 8 appetizer servings

- 2 large onions, peeled and cut in half
- 1 beef shank—ask your butcher to de-bone the shank (and give you the bones), cut the shank lengthwise into 4 pieces and trim of all fat. Each piece will be approximately 1 1/2 to 2 pounds after trimming.
- 1 head garlic, cut in half crosswise, plus 3 cloves, peeled and split
- 2 bay leaves
- 3 sprigs thyme
- 1/2 tablespoon coriander seeds
- 10 sprigs Italian parsley
- 1 teaspoon whole black peppercorns
- 4 medium leeks, green and white sections cut and separated
- 2 tablespoons coarse sea salt
- 8 quarts water
- 4 medium carrots, peeled and trimmed
- 4 stalks celery, peeled, trimmed and cut into 6-inch segments
- 4 turnips, trimmed and peeled
- 1 large tomato, cut in half and seeds removed
- Salt and freshly ground white pepper
- Eight 2-gram gelatin sheets
- One 4-ounce foie gras terrine, cut into 1/4-inch dice

1. Blacken the cut sides of the onions: Place the onions on a very hot flat surface, such as a griddle, and let cook until very burnt. If you don't have a griddle, place a very heavy pan, such as cast iron, over medium heat and then put the onions cut sides down in the pan. Cook until they are as dark as you can get them. Transfer the blackened onions to a plate.

2. In a deep stock pot, combine the blackened onions, beef shanks, shank bones, garlic, bay leaves, thyme, coriander seeds, parsley, peppercorns, green sections of the leeks, sea salt and water. The water should cover the beef by at least 5 inches. Add more water, if needed. Bring the water to a boil, then lower the heat and simmer for 3 hours, regularly skimming off the foam and any solids that rise to the surface. Remove the beef from the pot and set aside. Discard the vegetables, herbs, spices and bones. Strain the poaching liquid through a fine-mesh sieve.

3. Wash the pot and add the beef, carrots, celery, turnips, white sections of the leeks and tomato. Pour the reserved poaching liquid back in. Bring the liquid back to a boil, reduce the heat, and simmer for 1 hour, regularly skimming off the foam and any solids that rise to the surface. Discard the tomato and carefully remove the beef and vegetables from the liquid. Set aside and cool. When completely cooled, cut the beef and vegetables into 1/4-inch dice. Taste and season with salt and pepper, if necessary.

4. In a small bowl of cold water, soften the gelatin sheets. Lift the gelatin out of the water and squeeze it gently to remove excess moisture.

5. Prepare an ice-water bath in a large bowl and set aside. Strain the broth through a fine-mesh sieve into a bowl that will fit on top of the ice bath. Add the softened gelatin leaves to the hot broth and stir until dissolved. Taste and season with salt, if necessary. Place the bowl in the ice bath and stir until the broth becomes syrupy.

6. Over the bottom of a 8-ounce glass or shallow soup bowl, place a thin layer of the gelée. Top with 1 to 2 tablespoons of the diced vegetables. Add another thin layer of gelée to cover the vegetables and place a few pieces of foie gras and beef over the gelée. Repeat until the glass is three-quarters full. Finish with a thin layer of gelée to smooth out the top. Refrigerate for 1 hour to set.

For the Horseradish Cream:
- 1 cup heavy cream
- 1/4 cup freshly grated horseradish
- Salt and freshly ground pepper

In a small saucepan, bring the cream and horseradish to a boil. Lower the heat and simmer until the cream has reduced by half, about 10 to 15 minutes. Strain the cream through a fine-mesh sieve. Season with salt and pepper. Refrigerate until cool.

To Serve:
Season each serving with freshly ground pepper. Spoon the horseradish cream on top of the gelée and spread the cream to cover the entire surface using the back of a spoon. Serve immediately.

Wine selection
- Rioja (Spain)
  Sierra Cantabria Coeccion Privada 1999

6 6 This very dry Tempranillo based wine from northeast Spain balances the richness of the meat and aspic. The dry fruit and flower aromas of the wine also seem to add an extra layer of flavors to the dish. 9 9

"Jean-François Bruel and I both worked at Michel Guérard in France and we created this dish in reminiscence of the blend of rusticity and elegance. —DB"

117

Oxtail & Foie Gras Terrine

Makes 1 terrine

For the Oxtail:
- 8 pounds oxtail (3 tails), cut into 3-inch pieces
- Salt and freshly ground pepper
- 8 ounces (2 sticks) unsalted butter
- 3 stalks celery, scrubbed and roughly chopped
- 2 carrots, scrubbed and roughly chopped
- 1 medium onion, peeled and roughly chopped
- 1 head garlic, cut in half crosswise
- 1 small bunch Italian parsley
- 3 sprigs thyme
- 2 bay leaves
- Two 750 ml bottles dry red wine
- 16 cups unsalted beef stock or store-bought low-sodium beef broth
- 1/4 cup black truffle juice (optional)

1. Center a rack in the oven and preheat the oven to 300°F.

2. Generously season the oxtail pieces with salt and pepper. Melt 14 tablespoons of the butter in a Dutch oven or large casserole over medium-high heat. Add the oxtail and brown on all sides, turning as needed, approximately 30 minutes. Transfer the oxtail to a large platter and pour off any excess fat.

3. Melt the remaining 2 tablespoons butter in the same pan and add the celery, carrots, onion, garlic, parsley, thyme and bay leaves. Brown the vegetables lightly, stirring as needed, about 10 minutes. Add the wine and reduce until the pan is almost dry. Return the oxtail to the pan, pour in the beef stock and bring to a boil, skimming off the foam and any solids that rise to the surface. Season with salt and pepper. Cut a parchment paper circle to fit inside the pan and press it gently against the ingredients or cover the pan with its lid. Slide the pan into the oven and cook until the meat is very tender, 2 1/2 to 3 hours. Remove the pot from the oven.

4. Remove the meat; strain the liquid through a fine-mesh sieve. Discard the vegetables and herbs. While the oxtails are still hot, remove the meat from the bones and finely shred; discard the bones. Return the meat to the strained poaching liquid and stir in the truffle juice. Season well with salt and pepper.

For the Vegetables:
- 2 small carrots, peeled, trimmed and cut into 1/4-inch dice
- 1 small turnip, peeled, trimmed and cut into 1/4-inch dice
- 2 small stalks celery, peeled, trimmed and cut into 1/4-inch dice
- 2 globe artichokes
- 1 lemon, cut in half
- 2 tablespoons extra-virgin olive oil
- 1/2 pound black trumpet or white mushrooms, cut into 1/2-inch dice
- 1 clove garlic, peeled and crushed
- 1 sprig thyme
- Salt and freshly ground pepper

1. Bring a medium pot of salted water to a boil. Plunge the carrots, turnip and celery into the water and cook until tender, approximately 7 to 10 minutes. Transfer the vegetables to a colander and hold under cold running water. Drain well and pat dry.

2. Break off the stems of the artichokes. Using a very sharp knife, cut off all the large bottom leaves, leaving a cone of soft small leaves in the center. Pull them out by hand. Then, using a small knife and following the bowl shape of the artichoke hearts, trim away the fuzzy choke on top of the hearts. Trim off any green remaining on the side or bottom of the hearts. Cut the hearts into 1/2-inch thick slices and rub with the cut lemon.

3. Warm the olive oil in a large sauté pan over medium-high heat. Add the artichoke hearts, mushrooms, garlic and thyme, and season with salt and pepper; cook until the mushrooms are tender, approximately 4 to 5 minutes. Remove from the heat and discard the garlic and thyme. Strain the vegetables through a fine mesh-sieve. Set aside to cool.

To Assemble the Terrine:
- 3/4 pound fresh duck foie gras, sliced 1/2-inch thick, deveined and denerved (can substitute 1/2 pound of cooked foie gras terrine)
- Salt and freshly ground pepper
- Two (2-ounce) fresh or canned black truffles, thinly sliced

1. Season the foie gras with salt and pepper. Set a large heavy sauté pan over high heat and sauté the foie gras slices for 3 minutes on each side. Drain the foie gras on a plate lined with paper towels.

2. Line the inside of a 4- by 12 1/2-inch terrine mold (1 1/2- quart capacity) with plastic wrap, allowing it to extend over the sides. Place a 1-inch layer of oxtail meat and 1 cup of the oxtail poaching liquid in the bottom of the mold. Arrange half the vegetables in a layer on top of the meat and cover with half the black truffle slices. Arrange the foie gras over the truffle slices. Place the remaining vegetables on top and finish with another layer of oxtail meat. Pour the remaining 1 cup of oxtail poaching liquid over the terrine. Cover the terrine mold with plastic wrap and refrigerate for at least 8 hours or overnight.

To Serve: Unmold the terrine onto a cutting board and remove the plastic wrap. Using an electric or serrated knife, cut the terrine into 1-inch thick slices. Can be served with a side of mixed green salad with a mustard dressing.

Wine selection
- Anjou Quart de Chaume (France) Domaine des Baumard 1997

“While this wine is very rich, it has a focused acidity and mineral (wet stones) aromas that cut through the richness of the foie gras and oxtail.”

Roasted Sea Bass with Sweet Corn

Makes 4 servings

For the Sauce Diable:
- 2/3 cup dry white wine
- 1/4 cup white wine vinegar
- 3 shallots, peeled, trimmed and thinly sliced
- 1 sprig thyme
- 1/2 bay leaf
- 1 tablespoon whole black peppercorns, toasted and crushed
- 1 tablespoon demi-glace (or 1 cup unsalted beef stock reduced to 1 tablespoon)

In a small saucepan over high heat, combine the wine, vinegar, shallots, thyme, bay leaf and peppercorns. Cook until the mixture has thickened and reduced to 2 tablespoons. Stir in the demi-glace or reduced stock. Set aside and keep warm. The sauce should have a hot, peppery and acidic flavor.

For the Corn and Fava Bean Relish:
- 1/2 pound fava beans, shelled
- 1 tablespoon unsalted butter
- 1 clove garlic, peeled and crushed
- 1 sprig thyme
- 4 ears corn, shucked
- 1/4 pound bacon in one piece
- 3 tablespoons unsalted chicken stock or store-bought low-sodium chicken broth
- Salt and freshly ground pepper

1. Prepare an ice-water bath in a small bowl and set aside. Bring a large pot of salted water to a boil. Plunge the fava beans into the boiling water and blanch for 2 minutes. Drain and transfer to the prepared ice-water bath. Once cooled, drain and remove the skins of the beans. Rinse under cold running water and pat dry on paper towels.

2. Center a rack in the oven and preheat the oven to 350°F.

3. Using a large ovenproof sauté pan, cut out a parchment round large enough to cover the pan and set aside. Add the butter, garlic and thyme to the pan and cook over medium-high heat until the butter is light brown. Remove the thyme and add the corn and bacon. Cook, turning the corn occasionally, until slightly brown, about 10 minutes. Cover the pan with the parchment round and bake for 20 minutes, rotating the corn halfway through the baking. Remove the pan from the oven and discard the garlic; dice the bacon and set aside.

4. Holding an ear of corn on end, run a serrated knife down along the sides of the cob to remove the kernels. Repeat with the remaining corn and set aside.

5. Using a blender or food processor, purée one-fourth of the corn kernels with the chicken stock. Season with salt and pepper, set aside and keep warm.

For the Roasted Black Sea Bass:
- Four 6-ounce black sea bass fillets, skin left on
- 2 tablespoons extra-virgin olive oil
- Salt and freshly ground pepper
- 1 tablespoon unsalted butter

Using a boning knife, cut four 1/4-inch-thick slits across the top of the skin side of each fillet. (This will prevent the fish from curling.) Warm the olive oil in a large nonstick sauté pan over medium heat. Season the fillets with salt and pepper. Place the fish, skin side down, in the pan and cook until slightly browned, about 4 minutes. Turn the fillets over, add the butter and continue to cook for another 3 to 4 minutes. The fish is done when the flesh yields to slight pressure.

To Serve:
• 1 tablespoon extra-virgin olive oil

Warm the olive oil in a medium sauté pan over medium heat Cook the fava beans, corn, bacon, and 1 tablespoon of corn puree until heated through. Season with salt and pepper. Place the relish in the center of each warm dinner plate. Spoon the cornpuree around the relish and place a filet on top.

Drizzle a teaspoon of the sauce diable around the corn puree and serve immediately.

Wine selection
• Chablis Grand Cru "Blanchots Réserve de l'Obédiencerie" (France) Domaine Laroche 2000

“This bone-dry Grand Cru wine from northern Burgundy is quite powerful behind a veil of austerity. This makes it the perfect companion to the spices in the dish. The wine's acidity and mineral profile also combine well with the fish's texture.”

Moroccan Spiced Tuna with Carrots & Mint Oil

Makes 4 servings

For the Mint Oil:
- 1 bunch mint, leaves only
- 1 cup extra-virgin olive or grapeseed oil

1. Prepare an ice-water bath in a large bowl and set aside. Bring a medium saucepan of salted water to a boil. Plunge the mint into the boiling water and blanch until tender, 1 to 2 minutes. Transfer the mint to the prepared ice-water bath. Once cool, squeeze the leaves free of excess water.
2. In a blender, purée the mint leaves and oil together until the emulsion is bright green. Immediately strain the oil through a cheesecloth-lined sieve. Refrigerate until needed.

For the Vegetables:
- 2 tablespoons extra-virgin olive oil
- 3 spring onions, trimmed, peeled and each cut into 8 wedges
- 5 California carrots, peeled, trimmed and cut on the diagonal into very thin slices
- 10 cumin seeds
- 3/4 cup freshly squeezed orange juice
- 1 teaspoon thinly sliced Meyer lemon confit
- Salt and freshly ground pepper
- 5 sprigs cilantro

Warm the olive oil in a large sauté pan over medium-high heat. Add the onions and cook, stirring, until tender and translucent, 7 to 8 minutes. Add the carrots, cumin seeds and orange juice, reduce the heat to medium-low and continue to cook until the liquid has evaporated. Add the Meyer lemon confit and season with salt and pepper. Set aside and keep warm. Just before serving add the cilantro sprigs.

For the Tuna:
- 2 teaspoons zatar (Middle Eastern spice blend)
- 3/4 teaspoon coriander seeds
- 3/4 teaspoon fennel seeds
- 3/4 teaspoon cumin seeds
- 1/4 teaspoon paprika
- 1/4 teaspoon whole black peppercorns
- 1/4 teaspoon cayenne pepper
- 2 pounds yellowfin tuna loin (1-inch thick), divided into four pieces
- Salt
- 2 tablespoons extra-virgin olive oil
- Cooking oil

1. Finely grind the zatar, coriander seeds, fennel seeds, cumin seeds, paprika, peppercorns and cayenne pepper in a spice grinder.
2. Season the tuna first with the salt, then with the ground spices. Drizzle the olive oil over the tuna on both sides. Prepare a very hot grill. Brush the grill with the cooking oil, add the seasoned tuna and grill for 2 minutes on each side for medium-rare. Let the tuna rest for a minute before serving.

To Serve: **Divide and place the vegetables in the center of each warm dinner plate. Top with a tuna fillet and drizzle the mint oil around.**

Wine selection
- Hermitage Blanc (France)
  Domaine Jean-Louis Chave 1999

66 This wine is full bodied with aromas of white flowers and peach kernel that intermix nicely with the spices used in the recipe. The richness and roundness of the wine mesh well with the firmer texture of the tuna. 99

Sonora Skirt Steak with Three Sauces

Makes 4 servings

For the Mexican Salad:
- 1 poblaño chile pepper
- 1/4 cup extra-virgin olive oil
- 1 chayote, peeled, seeded and cut into 1/4-inch-wide strips
- 1/2 teaspoon Mexican oregano
- 1 napales cactus, cleaned and cut into 1/8-inch-wide strips
- 2 teaspoons freshly squeezed lime juice
- 1 large, ripe avocado, halved, pitted, peeled and thinly sliced crosswise
- 1/2 small red onion, thinly sliced
- 2 tablespoons chopped cilantro leaves
- Salt and freshly ground pepper

1. Preheat the broiler. Place the poblaño pepper onthe rack of a broiler pan and roast until the skin is half-charred. Cool the pepper and remove the charred skin and the seeds. Cut into thin strips.

2. In a medium sauté pan warm 1 tablespoon of the olive oil over medium heat. Add the chayote and oregano and cook, stirring occasionally, for 5 minutes. Add 1 more tablespoon olive oil and the cactus to the pan. Continue to cook, stirring occasionally, until the chayote and cactus are tender, about 8 to 10 minutes. Set aside to cool.

3. In a small bowl, whisk together the lime juice and remaining 2 tablespoons olive oil. Season with salt and pepper.

4. In a medium bowl, gently toss together the chayote, cactus, avocado, poblaño pepper, onion, cilantro leaves and lime vinaigrette. Season with salt and pepper. Cover and refrigerate until needed.

For the Mexican Crema Sauce (makes 3/4 cup):

- 3/4 cup fresh goat cheese, softened
- 1/4 cup plus 2 tablespoons sour cream
- Salt and freshly ground pepper

In a small bowl, mix together the goat cheese and sour cream until smooth. Add water, 1 tablespoon at a time, until a pourable consistency is achieved. Season with salt and pepper. Refrigerate until needed.

For the Salsa Verde (makes 1 cup):

- 1/2 pound tomatillos, husks and stems removed, rinsed well
- 1 small yellow onion, peeled, trimmed and sliced
- 4 cloves garlic, peeled
- 1 serrano chile pepper, halved, seeded and finely chopped
- 1 1/2 cups unsalted chicken stock or store-bought low sodium chicken broth, plus more if needed
- 1 cup cilantro leaves
- Salt and freshly ground pepper

In a small saucepan over medium-high heat, combine the tomatillos, onion, garlic, pepper and stock. Add additional stock to cover ingredients, if needed. Bring to a boil, reduce to a simmer and cook until the tomatillos and onions are tender, about 10 minutes. Remove from the heat and drain the liquid from the pan. Transfer the remaining ingredients to a blender or food processor; add the cilantro leaves and purée until smooth. Season with salt and pepper. Refrigerate until ready to use.

For the Chipotle Pepper Sauce (makes 3/4 cup):

- 1/2 pound tomatillos, husks and stems removed, and rinsed well
- 3 cloves garlic, unpeeled
- 1 ancho chile pepper
- 3 medium chipotle chile peppers
- 1 teaspoon Mexican ground cinnamon
- 1 teaspoon ground cumin
- 1/2 ripe mango, peeled and cut into large pieces
- Salt

1. Preheat the broiler. Roast the tomatillos under the broiler until the skin is half-charred. Cool the tomatillos and remove the charred skin.

2. Warm a small griddle, cast-iron pan or sauté pan over high heat. Add the garlic and roast until the skins are black, about 3 minutes, turning halfway through. Cool; remove the skins.

3. In the same pan over high heat, roast the ancho pepper until it smokes, about 2 minutes. Flip it over and roast until it smokes. Place the chile in a small bowl of warm water to rehydrate. Repeat the process with the chipotle peppers, roasting about 1 minute and rehydrating. Drain the chile and peppers, remove the seeds and set aside.

4. In the same pan, combine the cinnamon and cumin over medium heat. Shake the pan to prevent burning and roast until dry and fragrant, about 2 minutes.

5. In a blender, purée the tomatillos, mango, garlic, ancho chile pepper, chipotle chile peppers and spices until smooth. Season with salt.

For the Skirt Steak:
- 1 tablespoon extra-virgin olive oil
- One 10-ounce skirt steak, trimmed and cut into 4 equal portions
- Salt and freshly ground pepper
- 8 flour or corn tortillas

1. Warm the olive oil in a medium sauté pan or skillet over high heat until the oil smokes. Sear the steaks on both sides with salt and pepper and slip them into the pan. Sear the steaks for about 2 minutes on each side for medium-rare, 3 minutes per side for medium. Transfer the steaks to a heated platter and let rest for 3 minutes.

2. While the steak is resting, mist the tortillas with water and cook on a very hot griddle or in a sauté pan over medium-high heat until lightly charred, about 1 minute per side. Place the tortillas between damp towels or napkins. Thinly slice the steak against the grain of the meat.

Divide and arrange the steak among four plates along with the Mexican salad Serve with the tortillas and 3 sauces on the side.

Wine selection
- Maipo (Chile)
  Santa Rita "Reserva" Carmenère 1999

"This close relative of the Merlot grape grows very well in Chile. It's a smooth, medium bodied wine with gamey overtones that stands up very well against the grilled meat and its spicy sauces."

Goat Cheese Napoleon with Caramelized Quince

Makes 8 servings

For the Goat Cheese Filling:
- 1 1/2 two-gram gelatin sheets
- 1/2 cup whole milk
- 1/4 cup sugar
- One 7-ounce log fresh goat cheese

1. Soften the gelatin sheets in a small bowl of cold water. Lift the gelatin out of the water and squeeze gently to remove excess moisture.
2. Prepare an ice-water bath in a large bowl. In a medium saucepan, bring the milk and sugar to a boil. Add the gelatin and goat cheese and blend with an immersion blender. Cool the saucepan in the ice-water bath.
3. Place eighteen 1 1/2- by 1-inch ring molds on a parchment paper-lined baking sheet. Divide the mixture among the ring molds. Refrigerate until firm.
4. To remove, run a knife around the inside edges of the molds and gently push them out of the rings. Place on a parchment paper-lined baking sheet and refrigerate until needed.

For the Caramelized Quince:
- 6 cups water
- 1 1/2 cups sugar
- 1 star anise
- One 3-inch cinnamon stick
- 1/2 vanilla bean, split and scraped
- Juice of 1 lemon
- 3 quince, peeled and cut into 1/4-inch dice
- 4 tablespoons (1/2 stick) unsalted butter

1. In a medium pot, combine the water, sugar, star anise, cinnamon, vanilla bean seeds and pod and lemon juice and bring to a boil. Add the quince and poach at a simmer just until tender, 45 to 60 minutes. Remove from heat and let cool. Strain; reserve the poaching liquid and quince separately. Discard the spices and vanilla bean pod.

2. Melt the butter in a large sauté pan over medium-high heat. Add the quince and cook until it is a light golden brown. Add 2/3 cup of the reserved poaching liquid and reduce until the quince caramelizes. Let cool and set aside until needed.

For the Caramelized Phyllo:
- 1 1/4 cups freshly squeezed orange juice
- 1/3 cup strained apricot preserves
- 2 sticks plus 5 tablespoons (10 1/2 ounces) unsalted butter
- 4 sheets phyllo dough
- 1 3/4 cups confectioners' sugar

1. Center a rack in the oven and preheat the oven to 375°F. Line 2 baking pans with parchment paper and set aside.
2. In a small saucepan, bring the orange juice and apricot preserves to a boil and reduce by three-quarters. Gradually add the butter, stirring until smooth.
3. Place a phyllo sheet on the work surface and brush the sheet with some of the orange-butter mixture. Using a fine-mesh sieve or a sugar shaker sprinkle the phyllo with the confectioners' sugar. Place another sheet of phyllo on top and brush with more orange butter. Cut into twenty-four 3 1/2-inch triangles and arrange on the prepared baking pans. Repeat with the remaining phyllo sheets. Set aside the remaining orange butter. Bake the phyllo triangles until golden brown, about 6 minutes.

For the Apple Cider Granité:
- 4 cups fresh apple cider
- 1/2 cup sugar
- One 3-inch cinnamon stick
- 3 whole cloves
- 1/2 vanilla bean, split and scraped

In a large saucepan, combine the ingredients and bring to a boil. Using a fine-mesh sieve, strain the liquid into a loaf pan and place in the freezer. Stir occasionally with a fork until the liquid is frozen and granular.

To serve:
Place a phyllo triangle on a dessert plate. Spoon a small mound of quince compote on top of the phyllo. Place a goat cheese round on top. Repeat with another layer of phyllo, quince and goat cheese round. Top with a phyllo triangle and a scoop of granité. Drizzle the plate with the reserved orange butter.

Wine selection
- Poire Sparkling Pear Cider (France)
  Eric Bordelais

66 This fall preparation, high on taste and low on sugar, matches well with this Sparkling Pear Cider from Normandy. It's dry, elegant and just fizzy enough to spark up the dessert. 99

Caramelized Pineapple with Walnut Cake & Rum Sabayon

Makes 8 servings

For the Walnut Cake:
- 1 1/3 cups coarsely chopped walnuts
- 1/3 cup confectioners' sugar
- 3 tablespoons granulated sugar
- 3 large egg whites
- 3 tablespoons unsalted butter, softened

1. Center a rack in the oven and preheat the oven to 350°F. Butter the inside of a 6- by 2-inch round cake pan, dust with flour, tap out the excess, and place on a baking sheet.
2. In a food processor, pulse the walnuts, confectioners' sugar and 1 tablespoon of the granulated sugar until the walnuts are the consistency of fine crumbs. Do not overprocess. The mixture should not come together like a paste. Add 1 egg white and again pulse just until mixed. Add the butter and pulse just until mixed. The walnuts should still be in small pieces and there should be no emulsification. Transfer the mixture to a bowl.
3. In a bowl, whip the remaining 2 egg whites until the whites are broken up and foamy. Slowly add the remaining 2 tablespoons of sugar while whipping until the whites hold medium peaks. Fold the meringue into the walnut mixture.
4. Spoon the batter into the prepared pan and smooth the top with a spatula. Bake until the cake is golden brown and pulls away slightly from the pan, 25 to 30 minutes. Let the cake cool in the pan for 10 minutes, then unmold the cake and let cool on a wire rack.

Wine selection
- Vin Santo di Carmignano (Italy) Cappezzana "Riserva" 1996

For the Pineapple-Caramel Sauce:
- 3 tablespoons sugar
- 2 tablespoons light corn syrup
- 1/4 vanilla bean, split and scraped
- 1/2 cup fresh or canned pineapple juice

In a small saucepan over medium-high heat, combine the sugar, corn syrup and vanilla
bean seeds and pod and cook, stirring, until the sugar turns golden brown. Immediately deglaze with the pineapple juice and cook until the caramel has dissolved. Remove the vanilla bean pod and let the sauce cool.

For the Roasted Pineapple:
- 4 tablespoons (1/2 stick) unsalted butter, cut into small pieces
- 1/2 cup sugar
- 1 ripe pineapple, skin and core removed, cut into 8 wedges

Heat the butter in a large sauté pan over high heat until melted and foamy. Add the sugar and cook until the sugar turns golden brown. Add the pineapple and cook, making sure to roll the pineapple in the caramel to evenly coat each segment, until golden brown, approximately 10 to 12 minutes. Transfer the pineapple to a plate using a slotted spoon. Cut 4 or 5 partial slits into each segment, making sure not to cut through the pineapple. Set the pineapple aside.

For the Rum Sabayon (makes 1 1/4 cups):
- 1/4 cup heavy cream
- 4 large egg yolks
- 1/4 cup plus 1 tablespoon sugar
- 1/4 cup dark rum
- 1/4 vanilla bean, split and scraped

1. Whip the heavy cream in a bowl until it forms medium peaks. Refrigerate until needed.
2. Put the yolks, sugar, rum and vanilla bean seeds into the bowl of a mixer and set the bowl over, but not touching, simmering water. Cook, whisking constantly, until the mixture is warm to the touch and thickened, about 5 to 7 minutes. Remove the bowl from the heat and transfer the bowl to the mixer fit with the whisk attachment. Whip the sabayon on medium-high speed until it is cool to the touch, 4 to 5 minutes.
3. Fold the whipped cream into the sabayon.

" The combination of rum and walnuts in this cake works to the advantage of the Vin Santo, a wine with a high alcohol content and aromas of nuts, dried fruits and orange peels. The pineapple brings a nice zesty sensation to the wine . "

Place a large spoonful
of the sabayon in the center
of each plate.
Using the back of a spoon,
spread the sabayon
into a
circle.
Curve a pineapple segment
to the left of the
sabayon
circle.
Cut the walnut cake
into 8 pieces and
place one piece in the center
of each plate on top of the
sabayon. Lightly drizzle
the
caramel
sauce
over the cake.

Roasted Peaches with Lemon Thyme, Poppyseed Cake & White Peach Sorbet

Makes 6 servings

For the Roasted Peaches:
- 1/4 cup water
- 1/4 cup sugar
- 6 ripe medium peaches
- 12 sprigs lemon thyme

1. In a small saucepan over high heat, bring the water and 2 tablespoons of the sugar to a boil. Cook until the sugar has dissolved; set aside.

2. Center a rack in the oven and preheat the oven to 400°F. Butter the inside of an 8-inch square baking pan and set aside.

3. Prepare an ice-water bath in a large bowl and set aside. Bring a large pot of water to a boil. Gently lower the peaches into the boiling water and blanch for 30 seconds. Using a slotted spoon, transfer the peaches to the ice-water bath. When the fruit is cool enough to handle, drain on paper towels. Using a small paring knife, slip off the skins.

4. Place the peaches in the prepared pan and sprinkle with the remaining sugar and thyme sprigs. Bake for 10 minutes, remove from the oven, and brush the peaches with the sugar syrup, gently moving the peaches so they do not stick to the bottom of the pan. Continue to bake the peaches, basting every 5 minutes, until tender, about 10 minutes. The peaches should remain firm around the center but soft to the touch.

For the White Peach Sorbet:
- 3/4 cup water
- 1/2 cup sugar
- 2 cups white peach purée (or 4 large white peaches, skins removed, pitted and puréed in a blender)
- Juice of 1/2 lemon

Using a small saucepan over high heat, bring the water and sugar to a boil. Dissolve the sugar, add the peach purée and lemon juice, and stir to combine. Bring to a boil and remove from the heat. Transfer to a bowl and refrigerate until cool. Using an ice cream maker, process the sorbet according to the manufacturer's instructions. Place in a covered container and freeze for at least 1 hour before serving.

For the Poppyseed Cake:
- 8 tablespoons (1 stick) unsalted butter, softened
- 1/3 cup plus 1 tablespoon confectioners' sugar, sifted
- 4 large eggs, separated
- 3/4 cup almond flour
- 1/2 cup poppy seeds, ground
- 1 tablespoon honey
- Finely grated zest of 1/2 lemon
- 1/4 teaspoon ground cinnamon
- Pinch of salt
- 1/3 cup granulated sugar

1. Center a rack in the oven and preheat the oven to 350°F. Butter an 8- by 2-inch round cake pan, dust with flour and tap out excess; set aside.

2. In the bowl of a mixer fitted with a whisk attachment, cream the butter and confectioners' sugar on medium speed until light and pale. Add the egg yolks one at a time, mixing well after each addition. If the mixture appears to curdle, the butter is not soft enough: Continue to whip the batter until the butter softens and the mixture is smooth. Add the almond flour, poppy seeds, honey, lemon zest, cinnamon and salt and mix until combined. Transfer the mixture to a large bowl and set aside. Wash the whisk attachment and the bowl.

3. In the bowl of a mixer fitted with the whisk attachment, whip the egg whites on medium-low speed just until foamy. Increase the speed to medium-high and gradually add the granulated sugar. Continue to beat until the whites form stiff peaks. Using a rubber spatula, fold the meringue into the butter mixture. Do not worry about overfolding. The batter should be dense rather than light and fluffy.

4. Pour the batter into the prepared pan. Using an offset spatula, smooth the top. Bake until the cake is golden brown and pulls away from the sides of the pan, about 20 minutes. Cool in the pan on a wire rack for

10 minutes. Unmold the cake and cool completely on a wire rack. The cake will fall slightly as it cools.

Serve each roasted peach with a slice of cake and a scoop of white peach sorbet.

Wine selection
- Muscat de Baume de Venise (France) Domaine de Coyeux 2001

66 Sweet and round with a slight alcohol kick, this Muscat from the southern Rhône Valley echoes well the lemony flavors in the dish with nice peach and white flower aromas. 99

Chocolate Clafoutis

Makes 12 2 1/2-inch cakes

- 6 ounces bittersweet chocolate, chopped
- 4 tablespoons (1/2 stick) unsalted butter
- 3 large egg yolks
- 2 large egg whites
- 3 tablespoons sugar
- One 3 1/2-ounce package Droste white chocolate pastilles
- One 3 1/2-ounce package Droste bittersweet chocolate pastilles

1. Center a rack in the oven and preheat the oven to 375°F. Place twelve 2 1/2- by 1-inch ring molds on a lightly greased or parchment paper-lined baking sheet. Spray the rings with nonstick cooking spray.
2. Put the bittersweet chocolate and butter in a medium bowl. Set over a medium saucepan of simmering water, making sure the bottom of the bowl does not touch the water. Stir the chocolate and butter until melted. Remove from the heat and keep warm. The chocolate and butter can also be melted in the microwave oven on a low power setting at 10 second intervals.
3. In a small bowl, whisk the egg yolks until broken. Add the yolks to the chocolate mixture, stirring just until combined.

4. In the bowl of an electric mixer fitted with a whisk attachment, beat the egg whites on medium-low speed just until foamy. Increase the speed to medium-high and continue to whip the egg whites, adding the sugar gradually, until soft peaks form. Using a rubber spatula, fold the meringue into the chocolate mixture. The mixture should be overfolded to obtain a dense texture.
5. Fill the molds halfway with the chocolate batter, using about 1/4 cup for each. Place one white and one dark chocolate pastille on top of each clafoutis.
6. Bake until the clafoutis rise to the top of the molds, approximately 4 minutes. Using a spatula, transfer the rings to serving plates. Run a knife around the inside edges of the rings and carefully remove the molds. Serve warm.

Peach Scented Black Tea Truffles

Makes 5 dozen truffles

- 1 pound semi-sweet chocolate, finely chopped
- 2 cups heavy cream
- 1 ounce peach-scented black tea leaves (about 1/2 cup)
- 2 tablespoons unsalted butter, softened
- Cocoa powder, for rolling truffles

1. Place the chopped chocolate in a medium bowl and set aside.
2. Using a small pot, bring the cream to a boil. Remove from the heat, add the tea and infuse for 4 minutes. Strain the hot cream through a fine-mesh sieve over the chocolate. Using the back of a spoon, press the tea leaves to extract as much flavor as possible. Allow the cream to soften the chocolate for 2 minutes. Using a whisk, stir the ganache slowly until smooth. Avoid creating any air bubbles by stirring too quickly. Add the butter, stirring until incorporated. Transfer the ganache to a loaf pan. Cover with plastic wrap, making sure the plastic wrap touches the entire surface of the ganache. Refrigerate for several hours, until the ganache is set.
3. Place the cocoa powder in a shallow pie plate. Using a teaspoon dipped in hot water, hold the teaspoon perpendicular to the ganache and drag it across the surface, forming 1/2-inch balls. If the ganache becomes too soft, refrigerate as needed until set. Roll the truffles in cocoa powder and store in an airtight container in a cool place for up to three weeks.

Robert Parker
& Friends Wine Lunch

About six times a year we get together and have a blast. Robert Parker is the man who challenges me the most. He is one of the greatest gourmands of our time. He has an incredible passion for food and wine and he can write about it and talk about it. Also, he's one of the greatest supporters of French cuisine and wine. This lunch is a gathering of friends sharing wine and food, tasting some of the greatest wines of the century. It's informal, and yet it's a mega-thing, a big deal. It's pure decadence and love and passion for food and wine. —DB

Le Menu at Café Boulud	Les Grand Vins
VIETNAMESE SOUP	Château Haut Brion Blanc **1989**
TERRINE "MAISON"	
CEVICHE OF BLACK BASS	
PORCHETTA FAÇON NIÇOISE	
TRADITIONAL NEW ENGLAND CLAM CHOWDER	Laville Haut Brion Blanc **1985**
ROUGETS EN ESCABÈCHE	Laville Haut Brion Blanc **1985**
DUO OF AMERICAN BLUE CRAB	Domaine de Chevalier **1971**
soft shell crab with balsamic ramps	
zucchini blossoms stuffed with jumbo lump	
HOMEMADE SPAGHETTI	Château Lafleur **1982**
with cèpes, tomatoes and pecorino	Château L'Evangile **1982**
PANCETTA WRAPPED TUNA	Château Ausone **1976**
with pea coulis and spring truffle	Château L'Evangile **1975**
BABY LAMB FROM BIANCARDI	Château Lafleur **1966**
cooked five ways with zucchini eggplant and panisses	Château Latour **1960**
TARTINE OF SQUAB	Château Lafleur **1970**, Château Latour **1970**
"EN SALMIS"	Petrus **1970**, Hermitage La Chapelle Jaboulet **1961**
BRAISED SHORT RIBS OF BEEF	Château Haut Brion **1928**, Château L'Evangile **1947**
avec pommes mousseline	Vieux Château Certan **1948**
et carottes fondantes	
PLATEAU DE FROMAGES	Château Lafite Rothschild **1900**
	Château Margaux **1900**
MINI LEMON SOUFFLÉ	
EARLY SUMMER TART	
with plumcots, almonds and almond ice cream	

A Blast from the Past

Olivier Flosse, sommelier at Café Boulud

Mr. Big Jay, Ron Levine and Park smith

Robert Parker

Bob and I are both big fans of Côtes du Rhône wine and that's what we usually have when we get together to drink for pleasure.—DB

(from left to right): Steve Verlin,
Dr. Jerry Murphy, Andy Rahl and Daniel Oliveros

Tartine of Squab "en Salmis"

Makes 4 servings

- 4 squabs (14 to 16 ounces each), head removed, legs, wings, necks and backbone removed and reserved
- 4 tablespoons unsalted butter
- 1/4 cup cognac or brandy
- 2 cups unsalted chicken stock or store-bought low-sodium chicken broth
- 1 tablespoon sherry vinegar
- Salt and freshly ground pepper
- 1 tablespoon extra-virgin olive oil
- 1 pound wild mushrooms, trimmed, cleaned and thinly sliced
- 1 shallot, peeled, trimmed and thinly sliced
- Four slices sourdough bread
- 1 clove garlic, peeled and halved
- Four 2-ounce portions fresh foie gras

1. Center a rack in the oven and preheat the oven to 400°F.
2. Chop the wing, neck and back bones into small pieces. Melt 2 tablespoons of the butter in a large sauté pan over high heat. Add the bones and legs and cook until golden brown. Deglaze and flambé with the cognac and cook until the liquid has evaporated. Add the stock and lower the heat to a simmer; cook until the leg meat is tender, approximately 20 minutes. Remove the legs from the pan and let cool. Season the sauce with the vinegar, salt and pepper and reduce the liquid by half. Strain the sauce through a fine mesh sieve. Once the legs are cool enough to handle, remove the leg meat from the bones and finely chop.

3. In a large sauté pan over high heat, warm the olive oil. Add the mushrooms and shallot and cook until all the liquid in the pan has evaporated. Once cool, finely chop the mushroom mixture and combine with the braised leg meat. Season with salt and pepper.
4. Season the squab breasts with salt and pepper. In a large ovenproof sauté pan, melt the remaining 2 tablespoons of butter. Sear the breasts, skin side down, until golden brown. Flip the breasts over, place the pan in the oven and roast for 4 minutes. Remove the pan from the oven and place the squab on a wire rack to rest for a few minutes. Remove the breast meat from the bones and cut into thin slices. Set aside and keep warm.
5. Prepare a very hot grill. Rub the sliced sourdough bread with the cut garlic. Grill the bread on both sides to obtain a good, charred flavor. While the bread is grilling, warm a large sauté pan over medium-high heat. Season the foie gras with salt and pepper and cook for 3 minutes on each side. Drain on layers of paper towels.
6. Divide the mushroom-leg mixture evenly among the toasted sliced bread. Place a piece of foie gras on top of the mushroom mixture and place the sliced breast meat on top of the foie gras. Keep warm.

To Serve:
Warm the sauce, if necessary. Place the assembled bread slices on the center of four warm dinner plates. Spoon the sauce over the squab meat and around the plate.

Wine selection
- Priorat (Spain)
  Alvaro Palacios "Les Terrasses" 1998

66 The slight gaminess of this recipe works well with this Catalan wine with intense aromas of dark berries and mocha. The wine has a nice, round texture that coats the mouth, meshing well with the tartine. 99

we serve this dish
with a
mache salad
tossed in truffle
vinaigrette.

Desire in a Bottle

Serving the right wine to two hundred patrons is somewhat like trying to pick just the right birthday present for every member of your family. Actually, make that every member of twenty or thirty families. The gap between what we might say we want and what will make us happy varies from individual to individual. Multiply all of this by the number of courses in a meal and further amplify it by the wide range of sensitivity from person to person and you begin to grasp the complexities that confront the sommelier all through every service.

One more thing enters into the equation: price. You may want a Petrus '70 but be able to afford a Corihuela Zapata '96—both delicious wines, but one as expensive, relatively speaking, as a great painting, a race horse or a fickle lover, the other affordable and, in most cases, compatible with the same range of foods as the rare Bordeaux. Knowing what the customer wants in terms of taste and prestige of the label, the sommelier also serves another master the food.

A brawny short rib wants a wine with body, length and plenty of spice. Frog's legs transform themselves into something sublime when accompanied by a fruity, mineralized Chardonnay. Truffles love Côtes du Rhône. The flavor of grouse soars on a noble Burgundy.

3:00 p.m.

Jean-Luc Le Du tours vineyards around the world from
his computer, striking good deals with suppliers.

Funky cheeses adore a crisp Alsatian white. Chocolate tart
with raspberry sauce sparkles when paired with champagne
and wraps you in a dreamy dessert haze when enjoyed with
a port like a Ramos Pinto '63.

The choices are, if not truly endless, then virtually so. To the
afficianado of the wine game, food is something that exists
mainly for the purpose of challenging one's knowledge of wine.
Diners have been known to drop a hundred times more on their
wine bill than on dinner. More common, though, is the table that
wants to drink something that will enhance the meal but cost
less than a car payment. To fulfill the wishes, whims and wants
of so many, Daniel has a wine cellar of nearly 24,000 bottles.
He gets the "good stuff" from small bottlings and exclusive
vineyards and, just as important, from new winemakers that

don't have a big name yet but whose wine the sommelier snaps
up after one taste.

Golden, amber, bubbly, ruby red or yellow as diamonds
in firelight; thick or sweet, in glasses as wide as a baby melon
or as tall and thin as lovely legs in high heels—the variety of wine
experiences is nothing less than the many varieties of pleasure.

> *An important part of the wine program at our restaurants is educating the waitstaff.*
> *We often do comparative tastings to understand stylistic differences between the same grape*
> *grown in different terroir. For example, to learn how a reserved, mineral Chablis can be*
> *made from the same grape as a buttery, fruit-scented Chardonnay from the Barossa Valley*
> *in Australia. The wine class focuses on new and young wine rather than older, expensive*
> *wine, which is usually better established based on its reputation and vintage. We want*
> *the staff to learn about lesser-known wines from up and coming regions, new vintages*
> *and wine from affordable labels that can be easily recommended to our patrons. —DB*

Wine is a unique treasure of France. With wine you can taste history. As much as you wish you could taste Escoffier's food, you cannot. But you can drink the same wine that he drank. You can drink the same wine as some of the greatest people throughout history: Napoleon, Picasso, Pasteur, Matisse. Great old wine is not like a piece of art that you can keep looking at for centuries. Once you open the cork, it's over. You have to drink it. It's a bottled breath. —DB

3:30 p.m.

We eat first

Beet-Cured Salmon

Part of the fun in cooking is playing with recipes, tasting them and talking about them. It's a creative collaboration, a passing on of knowledge. One recipe inspires another, even if they don't all end up on the menu. This dish was prepared for us by John Raymond, a young extern at Daniel. He learned it from Pierre LeBlanc, one of his teachers at the Culinary Institute of America, and wanted to demonstrate it for us. It's a gravlax made with

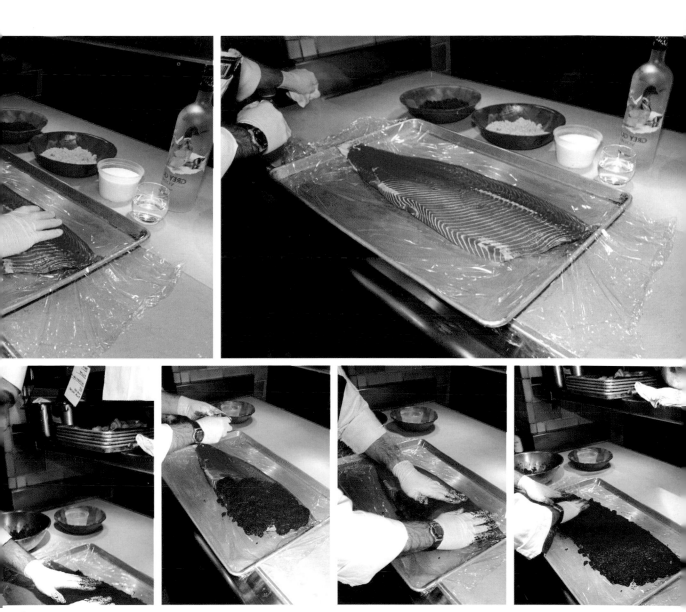

beets and vodka rather than dill. He covered the salmon with
fresh ground beets mixed with grated horseradish, vodka and,
of course, sugar, salt and pepper. After it had cured for two days,
the salmon flesh was dyed a pink-red from the beets. The entire
kitchen staff tasted it and I thought it was a very interesting
dish. We used some of it to make that evening's canapés.
Even a beginner chef, if he's motivated by cooking and by
what he's learned, can play a role in the kitchen. —DB

Steakhouse Pizza

Pizza has always been a favorite for family meals. The infinite array of toppings found in our kitchen makes it an adventure every time. This is especially true when boulanger Mark Fiorentino and sous chef Brad Thompson take over the preparation. If you had leftovers from Peter Luger's, the great old Brooklyn steakhouse, you could make this pizza. The recipe begins with thinly rolled dough, par-cooked until golden and brushed with garlic oil. Creamed spinach replaces the usual sauce, then the whole pie is put back

in the bread oven and cooked for a few minutes at 600° Fahrenheit. And then there's the meat—pink, juicy New York Sirloin, thinly sliced and arranged over the spinach like the spokes of a wheel, sprinkled with coarse salt and drizzled with horseradish cream. A final garnish of fried shallots tops it all off. The complex tastes meld together perfectly; shallots, sweated in butter, reduced cream and a pinch of nutmeg give the spinach a full, saucy flavor. The grated horseradish mixed with crème fraîche adds the ultimate kick. The staff devours it in minutes. —DB

Daniel Boulud and George Whipple

Marcia Stein, Citymeals-on-Wheels
executive director, Al Roker, NBC Today
Show, and Daniel Boulud

Citymeals-on-Wheels Event at Rockefeller Center

Chefs in America are very committed to giving back to the community. Citymeals-on-Wheels is one of the culinary world's charities of choice. And it's a great way to get together and have fun with colleagues from other restaurants—-it's kind of like a Woodstock for chefs! —-DB

4:30 p.m.

Chef Michel Richard, Chef Susan Spicer,
Daniel Boulud and Chef Dean Fearing

Chef Nobu Matsuhisa
and Daniel Boulud

DANIEL db BISTRO MODERNE CAFE BOULUD
MPANILE · LA BRE
Daniel Boulud
ancy Silver
NEW YORK

157

db Burger

I always thought I would love to intrigue my customers by making a burger at Daniel, but I had to make it the fanciest burger on earth. I was not going to make a burger without truffles and foie gras. The db burger had been something I'd had on my mind—like Georgia on my mind, you know?

Then one day a guy was talking to me about McDonald's, and about how when the French think of Americans it's all about burgers, and I said, "Well, it's because the French are jealous that they didn't invent the burger! As a Frenchman in America, my duty is to show you that we can make the greatest burger on Earth!" And I very quickly worked out this burger idea: foie gras, truffles, a little confit, short ribs braised in red wine, tomato and horseradish on a semolina bun with Parmesan. And a few pommes soufflés on the side, rather than French fries, out of nostalgia for the traditional French restaurants of old New York.

I wanted to create a burger that could go perfectly with red wine. Why? American burgers are made to go with beer more than red wine. I mean, for a classic burger, you want it to be charred outside, quite well, so you have a good flavor, then the bread is bland, the tomato is bland, you put on a little bit of ketchup and mustard, and it all goes very well with beer. It's the best. But my burger,with beer? No. With wine? Mmmm. It just elevates the thing, totally. —DB

You can play on the rusticity of the dish with a juicy Côtes du Rhône "Belleruche" 2000 from M. Chapoutier, a fruity wine with earthy scents and a spicy charm that's playful with the db burger. Or simply echo the richness of the meat patty with the opulent Château d'Aighuile 1999 from the Côtes de Castillon, an up-and-coming appellation satellite of St. Emilion. This wine is made by the same team that oversees Canon La Gaffelière and La Mondotte and has seductive aromas of dark berry, mocha and cinnamon.

159

Rocky Road Ice Cream Sandwich

Makes 24 individual sandwiches

For the Chocolate Brownies:
- 1/2 cup plus 2 tablespoons all-purpose flour
- 1/2 cup plus 2 tablespoons cocoa powder, preferably Dutch-process
- 1 1/2 cups sugar
- 1/4 teaspoon salt
- 3 large eggs
- 12 tablespoons (1 1/2 sticks) unsalted butter, melted and kept hot
- 3/4 cup chopped walnuts

1. Center a rack in the oven and preheat the oven to 350°F. Grease a 9- by 13-inch baking pan with nonstick cooking spray and set aside.

2. Sift together the flour and cocoa powder.

3. In a large bowl, whisk together the sugar, salt and eggs. Add the hot melted butter. Add the sifted dry ingredients and walnuts and mix just until incorporated.

4. Pour the batter into the prepared pan and bake until a knife inserted into the center comes out clean, 18 to 20 minutes. Place the pan on a wire rack and cool completely. Unmold the brownie from the pan, keeping it in one piece. Line the brownie pan with plastic wrap, allowing the plastic to extend over the sides. Return the brownie to the pan and freeze. (Can be made up to one week ahead and kept frozen.)

For the Rocky Road Ice Cream:
- 2 cups whole milk
- 2 cups heavy cream
- 1/2 cup sugar
- 8 large egg yolks
- 12 ounces bittersweet chocolate, finely chopped
- 3/4 cup slivered almonds, toasted
- 1 1/2 cups mini marshmallows
- Brownies (from above)

1. In a small saucepan over high heat, combine the milk, cream and 1/4 cup of the sugar and bring to a boil.

2. Prepare an ice-water bath in a large bowl and set aside. In a medium bowl, whisk the remaining 1/4 cup sugar and egg yolks together until light and pale.

Gradually pour half the hot milk mixture over the yolks while whisking constantly. Pour the mixture back into the saucepan. Cook over medium heat, stirring constantly with a wooden spoon, until the mixture thickens and coats the back of the spoon, 3 to 4 minutes. Strain through a fine-mesh sieve into a medium bowl. Add 7 ounces of the chocolate and stir until the chocolate has melted. Place the bowl in the ice-water bath and cool completely.

3. Put the remaining 5 ounces of chocolate into a medium bowl set over a pan of simmering water, making certain that the bottom of the bowl does not touch the water. Stir occasionally with a rubber spatula until the chocolate is melted and hot. Remove from the heat. Toss in the almonds and stir until the nuts are completely coated with the chocolate. The chocolate can also be melted in a microwave oven using low power, at 10 second intervals, stirring frequently.

4. Remove the brownies from the freezer. Using an ice cream maker, process the ice cream according to the manufacturer's instructions. Working very quickly, fold the marshmallows and the chocolate covered almonds into the ice cream and spread the ice cream evenly over the brownie. Cover the pan with plastic wrap and place in the freezer until the ice cream is firm, 1 to 3 hours.

For the Streusel:
- 12 tablespoons (1 1/2 sticks) unsalted butter, cut into small pieces
- 1 3/4 cups almond flour
- 1 1/4 cups all-purpose flour
- 1 cup sugar
- 1/2 teaspoon salt

1. In the bowl of a food processor fitted with the steel blade attachment, mix all of the ingredients together until a dough forms. Divide the dough in half. Form half of the dough into a small square block and refrigerate until firm. Roll the remaining dough between two pieces of plastic wrap into a 9- by 13-inch rectangle. Transfer the rectangle to a baking sheet, cover with plastic wrap and refrigerate until the dough is firm, about 1 hour.

2. Using a box grater or a cooling rack, coarsely grate the chilled streusel block into small crumbs. Set aside.

3. Center a rack in the oven and preheat the oven to 350°F.

4. Cut the chilled streusel rectangle into 24 equal squares and, using a flat or offset spatula, transfer the squares to a parchment paper-lined baking sheet, spacing the cookies 1-inch apart. (The cookies will spread a little.) Sprinkle some of the crumbled streusel on top of each square. Bake the streusel squares until golden brown, 11 to 13 minutes. Let the cookies cool on the baking sheet for 3 to 5 minutes. Carefully transfer the cookies to a wire rack and cool completely.

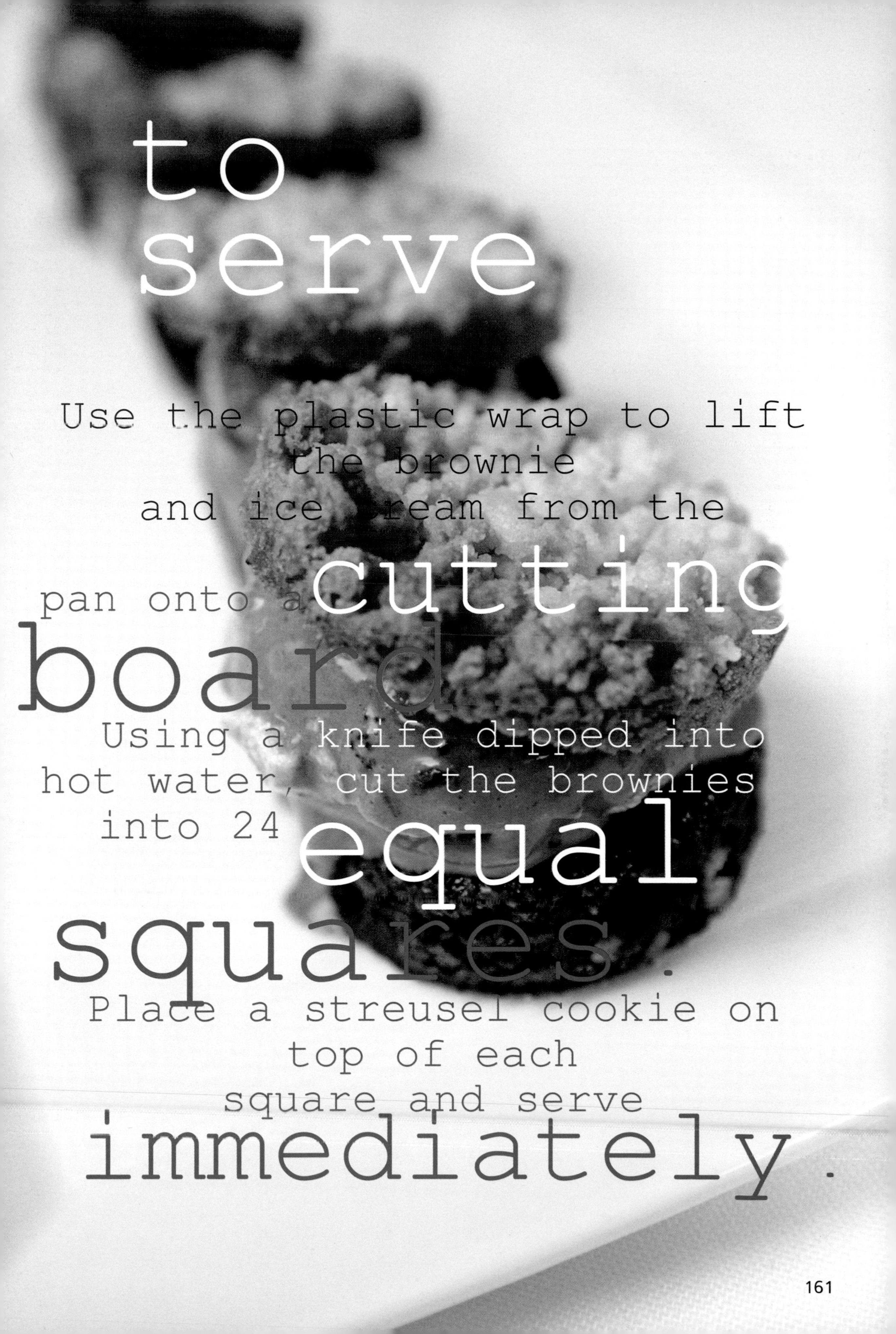

to serve

Use the plastic wrap to lift
the brownie
and ice cream from the

pan onto a cutting

board.

Using a knife dipped into
hot water, cut the brownies
into 24 equal

squares.

Place a streusel cookie on
top of each
square and serve

immediately.

Rosemary Braised Veal Shank

Makes 4 servings

- 1 veal shank, about 2 pounds (ask your butcher to trim the top and bottom bones)
- 1 tablespoon salt
- 1/2 teaspoon freshly ground black pepper
- 4 sprigs rosemary, cut to the same length as the shank
- 5 tablespoons extra-virgin olive oil
- 2 large Spanish onions, peeled, trimmed and cut into 1/2-inch thick wedges
- 6 cloves garlic, peeled and sliced
- 4 stalks celery, peeled, trimmed and cut on the bias into 1/2-inch-thick slices
- 2 large carrots, peeled, trimmed and cut on the bias into 1/2-inch thick slices
- 1 leek, white and light green parts only, sliced and cut on the bias into 1/2-inch thick slices
- 1 tablespoon tomato paste
- 1 tablespoon whole black peppercorns, crushed
- 2 bay leaves
- 1/2 tablespoon all-purpose flour
- 2 cups dry white wine

- 8 cups unsalted beef stock or store-bought low-sodium beef broth
- 1 large tomato, peeled, seeded and cut into 1/2-inch cubes

1. Center a rack in the oven and preheat the oven to 350°F.

2. Season the shank with the salt and pepper. Use kitchen twine to tie the shank in 1-inch intervals. Tuck in the rosemary sprigs.

3. Warm 3 tablespoons of the olive oil in a Dutch oven or casserole over high heat. Slip the meat into the pan and brown it evenly, turning it carefully as needed until all the surfaces of the meat are a light golden brown. Transfer the shank to a platter and let rest.

4. Warm the remaining 2 tablespoons olive oil in the same pan over medium heat. Add the onions, garlic, celery, carrots and leek and cook until the vegetables are tender but have no color, approximately 8 to 10 minutes. Add the tomato paste, peppercorns and bay leaves and cook for 2 minutes more. Stir in the flour, then add the the shank, wine, stock and tomato. Bring the liquid to a boil and cover the pot with a lid. Slide the pot into the oven and braise until the shank is very tender, about 2 hours.

5. Transfer the meat to a heated serving platter. Cut off and discard the kitchen twine and rosemary. Boil the pan liquid until it reduces by three-quarters. Strain the sauce over the meat and serve immediately.

I learned about catering when I was very young. As an apprentice in Lyon, I cooked for presidents and celebrities in their private homes or in the town hall. This aspect of the business always fascinated me. It's like belonging to a circus that's taking its act on the road. It teaches you improvisation, which is a must in order to succeed.—DB

Wine selection
- Santa Maria Valley Pinot Noir, California (U.S.) Byron 1998

66 Light bodied, with cinnamon and red-berry aromas that pair well with the carrots and turnips. The vivacious nature of this wine with high acidity enlivens the slowly braised veal shank. 99

All Is Ready

Now, in the quiet of late afternoon, is the midpoint, the fulcrum of the day when the shopping, the chopping, all the preparation tips over into service. This is the eye of the daily storm. The morning's whirlwind foreshadowed the approaching tempest. Soon, when the first diners are seated, the storm will return.

The massive ranges send up shimmers of heat like the wavy image of a desert mirage. Enough BTUs to warm the hearths of a small village. The diced vegetables—every piece tiny and identical to its neighbor or there will be hell to pay. The pans all stacked, all clean. Likewise, aprons spotless as bridal gowns.

5:30 p.m.

Lamb shoulders, braised and pulled. Terrines of foie gras, oysters cleaned of sand waiting to be shucked, still pulsing water through their glistening flesh. The bass, sheathed in potato slices, each piece of fish exactly 3 by 6 inches. The sauces, seasoned, re-seasoned, tasted, and seasoned again. The saucier says they are balanced. Daniel tastes to make sure he agrees. "Almost, but not exactly," he says. He salts, peppers, swirls and tastes. Nothing is ever perfect—but at every service you start out believing it will be.

RESTAURANT

Time

RM SVC

BAR

Room Inquiry

PC-UWS #4

The only sound is the hiss of flame, a low note like a breeze in the willows. Outside, on the sidewalk, the crew gathers for a last gab. A few smoke cigarettes. Many of the French still consider tobacco a vegetable. The first of the town cars, black and polished mirror-smooth, pulls up to the front door. Elegant swing of coutured leg, crease of trouser, sparkle of golden earrings. And always a certain smile . . . the one you get when you look at a handful of aces, the one food and wine lovers wear when they anticipate great pleasure.

DANIEL

	Enter/ Yes	Clear/ No	Trans Cancel
	7	8	9
	4	5	6
	1	2	3
Help	.	0	Send

"Daniel is the restaurant I've dreamed of ever since I was a young chef working in three-star restaurants in France. I always wanted to have a French restaurant that was equal to my mentors'. A restaurant that belonged among the great restaurants of the world. I wanted a restaurant that reflected my entire career, everything I've worked for, which has been to achieve the best food, the best service, the best atmosphere.

I want Daniel to keep evolving, to keep getting better. I'm inspired by New York City, by the great institution that it is, and it's what really drives me. I want Daniel to be a part of the history of great French food in New York, to be in the chapter of the great French restaurants of this city."

—DB

Dinner Service

Much has been written about the mayhem in a kitchen during service. True, to the outsider, it is all clatter, shouting, high-speed shaking of pans, showering of garnish, plating and pickup. But on second look the wonder is not the frantic pace, the staccato drill sergeant commands of the chef. What is truly remarkable about a restaurant kitchen is that it all moves so smoothly.

One hundred diners going through a procession of courses. At each table a coming together of processes that start at different times with different ingredients. Like airplanes from around the world converging on a big city airport: The roast that took three hours and the tuna that was seared for minutes, the raw oyster and the poached foie gras, the long simmered soup and the flash-fried scallop, all arrive at the table at exactly the same time. A restaurant is not just a kitchen and a dining room. A restaurant is a process, a piece of software, a way of organizing the efforts of scores of people and hundreds of ingredients and having them all come together as if nature decreed it.

The fury of the kitchen belies its inexorable orderliness. Its manic energy is just the yin to the languorous yang of the dining room. Adrenaline rush versus Zen calm. The chef takes his pleasure in speed and action, the patron in slow delectation. For every pungent expletive hurled at a slowpoke sous-chef there is a balancing sigh of sensual ecstasy as some morsel is tasted at table.

When Daniel puts on a new starched white tunic and makes the rounds of the dining room, it is as if his personality is transformed with the swinging of the door that separates the kitchen from the front of the house. The metallic banging of stove and steel gives way to the subtle click and scrape of silver on china. The shouts on the line yield to the susurrus of the carpeted salon. And Daniel—who just minutes ago was all about concentration, speed and the occasional burst of anger (or at least unrestrained encouragement) —now must glide around the room and smile. He must listen fully to each diner he chats up. This is their moment to feel that the entire institution is geared to afford them pleasure. Though Daniel is aware of the rest of the room, he must really listen, really respond and be charming and funny, lest he look as if he is going through the motions. A restaurateur must make everyone, man and woman, feel like the most desirable girl at the prom.

The field marshal in the kitchen, the perfect host in the dining room. The chef restaurateur could not be more of a split personality. That may explain why the great ones, or even just plain good ones, are so rare.

Alex Lee

My first encounter with Alex was at Macy's: I was doing a cooking demonstration, and Alex was in the audience. Afterward he came up to me and told me that he'd like to work with me one day. Within a month, he had a job at Le Cirque. After two years there, he was very serious about his craft and very dedicated to learning French cuisine. You can tell a lot about someone by how precise, consistent and disciplined he or she is. Alex had the magic touch of a real chef, that certain something extra that makes a chef good every time.

At this point he asked me if I could help him get a position working at Ducasse in Monte Carlo. Alex had made the commitment to save money to spend on his education, so I called Ducasse and told him that I had a talented young American who would work for him for six months for free. After a few months, Ducasse started paying him because he was doing such a good job. Alex worked many different stations there and spent his free time working with the baker, the pastry chef and the butcher. He learned French, visited every possible market, sampled every available delicacy and really took advantage of his time there. He went to Italy to the Santini family at Dal Pescatore and spent some time with Arzak in Spain as well.

A year and a half later he came back to the States, around the time that I was opening Daniel. I needed a good chef de cuisine and I preferred to open my New York restaurant with a French-trained American chef rather than an American-trained French chef. Alex has a great sensibility for French

cuisine and an amazing capacity to adapt other cuisines to create delectable combinations. He has an encyclopedic knowledge of food and is an excellent teacher. Even though he had never been a sous chef or a chef before, I was sure he had immense potential. And it's really worked out—he's been a great asset to the kitchen at Daniel ever since. —DB

Dinner at Daniel

6:00 p.m.

With the lifestyle of New York City, there is nothing better than cocktail time, when you know you can just drop everything and have a good drink. It's people's daily medicine, gets them a little smoother around the edges. In the lounge at Daniel—where people gather after work, couples meet, friends get together—it's when the night begins. I get excited coming up with cocktail recipes—they're not as complex as cooking, they're mostly a balance of tastes, but they're very interesting. It definitely takes a motivated and very good bartender to create a very good cocktail. —DB

Hibiscus Marteani

```
1 tablespoon water
1 tablespoon sugar
1/2 ounces Hibiscus tea
3 1/2 ounces Absolut Citron
```

1 Combine the water and sugar in a small saucepan over high heat. Stir until the sugar is dissolved. Let cool

2 Combine 1 teaspoon of the simple syrup from above with the other ingredients. Shake all ingredients over ice together and strain into a chilled martini glass.

db Mule

2 ounces

vodka

1/2 ounces Canton

ginger liquor

Splash Roses lime juice

ginger ale

Shake the vodka, ginger

liquor and lime juice

together and pour into a

glass

with ice. Top off with

ginger ale.

"hulla-[1] boulud"[2] martini

- 1 tablespoon water
- 1 tablespoon sugar
- 2 ounces Sauza tequila
- 1/2 ounces Triple Sec
- Splash prickly pear purOe
- 2 tablespoons freshly squeezed limejuice

1. Combine the water and sugar in a small saucepan over high heat. Stir until the sugar is dissolved. Let cool

2. Dip the rim of a chilled martini glass into prickly pear purOe and lime juice, then into granulated sugar.

3. Shake all the ingredients together over ice and strain into the martini glass.

Prosciutto & Parmesan Gougeres

Makes about 7 dozen hors d'oeuvres

- 8 tablespoons (1 stick) unsalted butter, cut into small pieces
- 1 cup water
- 1/2 teaspoon salt
- 1/4 teaspoon sugar
- 1 1/2 cups all-purpose flour

- 6 large eggs plus 1 lightly beaten egg
- 1 cup grated Parmesan cheese
- 1/2 cup prosciutto (about 2 ounces), finely chopped
- Pinch of freshly grated nutmeg
- Pinch of paprika

1. Center a rack in the oven and preheat the oven to 400°F.

2. In a medium saucepan, combine the butter, water, salt and sugar and bring to a boil. Immediately remove from the heat and add the flour, beating vigorously with a wooden spoon until smooth. Place the pan over high heat and cook, stirring continuously, until a smooth mass forms and the bottom of the pan is coated with a thin crust, about 2 minutes.

3. Transfer the batter to the bowl of an electric mixer fitted with the paddle attachment. Add the 6 eggs, on medium speed, one at a time, mixing well after each addition. Add the Parmesan, prosciutto, nutmeg and paprika.

4. Using a pastry bag fitted with a 1/2-inch round tip, pipe the batter onto parchment paper-lined baking sheets, forming mounds about 3/4-inch in diameter. Lightly brush with the beaten egg, smoothing the top surface with wet fingers. Bake at 400°F for 15 minutes, reduce the oven to 375°F and continue baking until puffed and golden brown, about 20 minutes. Transfer the gougères to a wire rack, cool slightly and serve warm.

Wine selection
• Barbera d'Asti "Tre Vigne" (Italy) Vietti 1997

66 This Italian take on the traditional Burgundian gougère matches well with this medium-bodied high toned Barbera from one of the old masters from Piedmont 99

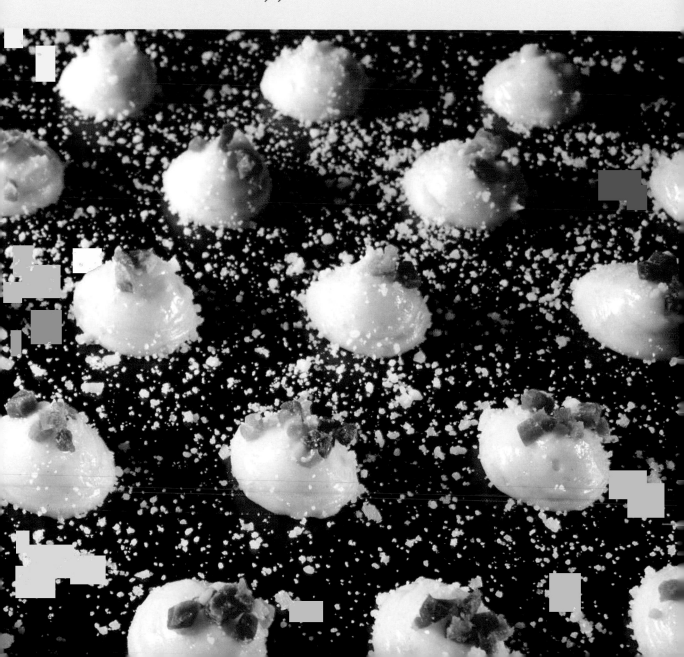

Maine sea scallop
ceviche with sea urchin
caviar and celery

Little Bites or Canapes

They're about the pleasure
of eating with your fingertips—it's taking a formal dish
and concentrating it into
something very small.

**I can take a whole
bouillabaisse**
and put the taste in a little
tartlet. It's shrinking a great
recipe into one bite. —DB

Bluefin tuna in mustard
oil dressing wrapped in a pink
radish and tied with a chive

Peeky toe crab
and mango wrapped
in a cucumber slice

Pea Pomponnette

Makes 5 dozen hors d'oeuvres

For the Pâte Brisée:
- 1 cup plus 3 tablespoons all-purpose flour
- 6 tablespoons cold unsalted butter, cut into small pieces
- Pinch of salt
- 1 large egg, lightly beaten

1. In the bowl of a food processor fitted with the steel blade attachment, combine the flour, butter and salt. Pulse just until the ingredients are crumbly and the size of small peas. Add the beaten egg and pulse just until the mixture is moistened. Do not overprocess the dough. Form two discs of equal size, wrap in plastic wrap and refrigerate for at least 1 hour.

2. Butter and flour thirty 1 1/2-inch round tartlet molds (if available, use nonstick molds); set aside. On a clean lightly floured work surface, roll one disc of dough out to 1/8-inch thickness. Using a 2-inch round cutter, cut out 30 circles of dough. Press the dough into the bottom and against the sides of the molds. Using a small paring knife, trim away any excess dough. Place the molds on a baking sheet and refrigerate the tartlet shells for 30 minutes.

3. Center a rack in the oven and preheat the oven to 350°F.

4. Cut out thirty 2-inch rounds of parchment paper. Place the rounds inside each mold and fill with dried beans or pie weights. Bake for 10 to 12 minutes, rotating the pan halfway through the baking process. Do not allow the dough to color. Place on a wire rack, cool completely, and remove the beans or weights and parchment paper. Repeat the process with the remaining dough.

For the Pea Filling:
- 1/2 pound assorted fresh peas and beans, such as English peas, fava beans, sugar snap peas and snow peas
- 2 tablespoons heavy cream
- 1 large egg
- 1 large egg yolk
- Salt and freshly ground pepper
- 1 ounce Parmesan cheese
- 8 chives, chopped

1. Shell the English peas and fava beans if using. Thinly slice the sugar snap peas and snow peas if using.

2. Center a rack in the oven and preheat the oven to 350°F.

3. Bring a medium pot of salted water to a boil. Cook the sugar snap peas and snow peas for 3 minutes. Add the English peas and cook for another 3 minutes. Put the fava beans in a strainer or colander and lower into the boiling water; cook for 2 minutes. Lift out the strainer; drain the remaining peas. Cool all the beans and peas under cold running water and drain

again. Remove the skins of the fava beans.

4. Put the peas, fava beans and heavy cream in a blender and purée until smooth, using a rubber spatula to scrape down the sides as needed. Add the egg and yolk and mix until combined. Season with salt and pepper. Transfer to a 2-cup liquid measure or other vessel with a pour spout.

5. Using a vegetable peeler, shave the Parmesan into small strips and set aside.

6. Place the prebaked tartlet shells on a parchment paper-lined baking sheet. Fill the tartlet shells with the pea filling. Bake until the custard is just set, 6 to 8 minutes. Cool slightly on a wire rack. Sprinkle with the chopped chives and top with a piece of shaved Parmesan. Can also be garnished with oven-dried ham or sautéed Hon Shimeji or morel mushrooms. Serve warm.

Pea pomponnette

Wine selection
- Vouvray Pétillant "Brut" (France) Domaine Foreau Non Vintage

> A light dry sparkling wine is a nice counterpoint to the creamy texture of this canapé. This version made from Chenin Blanc grapes in the Loire Valley jazzes up the dish with its lemony aromas.

Tomato Confit

Makes about 4 dozen hors d'oeuvres

For the Tomato Confit:
- 10 ripe plum tomatoes
- 2 cloves garlic, peeled, split and finely sliced
- 5 basil leaves, torn
- 2 sprigs thyme, leaves only
- 1 bay leaf, crushed
- 2 tablespoons extra-virgin olive oil

- Salt and freshly ground pepper
- 1/2 teaspoon sugar

1. Prepare an ice-water bath in a large bowl and set aside. Bring a large pot of water to a boil. Using a small paring knife, cut a small "x" on the bottom of each tomato. Place the tomatoes in boiling water for 30 seconds. Using a slotted spoon, immediately remove and place in the ice bath to cool.
2. In a small bowl, combine the garlic, basil, thyme and bay leaf and set aside.
3. Center a rack in the oven and preheat the oven to 200°F. Line a baking sheet with parchment paper and spread 1 tablespoon of the olive oil over the pan. Sprinkle with the salt and pepper and half the garlic herb mixture.
4. Using a small paring knife, peel the tomatoes. Cut the tomatoes in half lengthwise and remove the center membrane and seeds. Lay the tomatoes cut side down on the prepared pan. Brush the tops of the tomatoes with the remaining olive oil and season with salt, pepper and sugar. Sprinkle with the remaining garlic herb mixture.
5. Bake the tomatoes until very tender, about 2 1/2 hours, turning the tomatoes over halfway through the baking process. Open the oven door every 30 minutes or so to get rid of the moisture. Cool the tomatoes to room temperature.

Assembling the Tomato Confit Roulade:
- Tomato Confit (see recipe above)
- 12 basil leaves
- 1/4 pound fresh mozzarella cheese,
  cut into 1/2- by 1/2- by 2 1/2-inch sticks
- Salt and freshly ground black pepper
- 1/4 cup black olive tapenade

1. Lay a 10-inch piece of plastic wrap on a flat work surface. Place 6 tomato halves in a row, touching side by side. Lay 4 tomato halves, touching end to end, at the top of the tomato row, to form half a rectangle about 3 1/2 inches by 8 inches. Repeat with the 10 remaining tomato halves to form a rectangle. Lay 3 large basil leaves, end to end, down the center of the tomato rectangle. Place 3 mozzarella sticks, end to end, down the center of the basil leaves. Season with salt and pepper. Spread 2 tablespoons of tapenade over the mozzarella and lay 3 large basil leaves, end to end, on top.
2. Starting on the long edge of the rectangle, use the plastic wrap to tightly roll the tomato confit away from you, forming a log. Roll the log in the plastic wrap and twist the ends of the plastic wrap tightly to compact the roll. The log should be about 1 inch in diameter. Repeat the process with the remaining ingredients to form a second log. Freeze for 2 hours.

For the Garlic Croutons:
- 1 large head of garlic
- 3 tablespoons extra-virgin olive oil
- Salt and freshly ground pepper
- 1 French baguette, no more than 1 1/4 inch in diameter
- 3 sprigs thyme, leaves only, finely chopped
- 2 sprigs rosemary, leaves only, finely chopped

1. Center a rack in the oven and preheat the oven to 375°F. Line a baking sheet with parchment paper and set aside.
2. Cut the unpeeled head of garlic in half crosswise. Drizzle each cut side with 1/2 tablespoon olive oil and season with salt and pepper. Place on the baking sheet cut side down and bake until the cloves are tender and pop out of their skin when squeezed, about 30 minutes. Remove the skin and mash the cloves into a paste.
3. Reduce the oven temperature to 350°F. Line a baking sheet with parchment paper. Spread the garlic paste on top of the baguette. Using a serrated knife, cut the baguette into 1/8-inch thick slices, about 48 slices. Place the slices on a baking sheet and brush with the remaining 2 tablespoons olive oil. Sprinkle with the chopped thyme and rosemary and season with salt and pepper. Bake until the croutons are a light golden brown, about 4 to 5 minutes, and cool completely.

To Serve:
- 1/4 cup black olive tapenade
- 2 tablespoons extra-virgin olive oil

Line a baking sheet with parchment paper. Remove the tomato confit roulade from the freezer and unwrap. Using a serrated knife, cut each tomato roll into 1/4-inch thick slices, about 24 pieces per roll, and place on the baking sheet. Allow the slices to come to room temperature. Spread the garlic croutons with tapenade, top with a slice of roulade, and brush lightly with olive oil. Serve immediately.

Wine selection
- Santa Ynez Valley, California (U.S.)
  Verdad Albari Ibarra-Young Vineyard 2000

66 Of Spanish descent, the Albario grape is now planted in the Central Coast of California. In this setting, it produces wines that are high toned and perfumed, a nice foil for the Provençal elements in this dish 99

Tomato confit

Fennel Risotto Balls with Piquillo Pepper Coulis

Makes 50 hors d'oeuvres

- 1 fennel bulb, leaves separated and bulb cut into 1/8-inch dice
- 1 bunch Italian parsley, leaves only
- 7 cups unsalted vegetable stock or store-bought low-sodium vegetable broth
- 8 tablespoons (1 stick) unsalted butter
- 1 small onion, peeled, trimmed and cut into 1/8-inch dice
- 2 cups Arborio rice
- Salt and freshly ground pepper
- 1/2 cup freshly grated Parmesan cheese
- 1/4 pound fontina cheese, cut into small pieces
- 1 tablespoon mascarpone cheese
- 1 tablespoon fennel seeds, toasted
- 1 tablespoon Pastis or other anise liquor
- Piquillo Pepper Coulis (from page 59)
- 1/2 cup all-purpose flour
- 2 large eggs, lightly beaten
- 1 cup bread crumbs
- Peanut oil for deep-frying

1.   Bring a medium pot of salted water to a boil. Plunge the fennel leaves into the boiling water and blanch for approximately 5 minutes. Add the parsley and cook for 1 minute longer. Drain and hold under cold running water to stop the cooking. Squeeze the leaves to remove the excess moisture.   In a blender, purée the fennel and parsley leaves together until the emulsion is bright green. Set aside.

2.   Bring the stock to a boil in a large saucepan. Reduce the heat to medium-low and keep the stock at a slow, steady simmer.

3.   Melt the butter in a Dutch oven or large casserole over medium heat. Add the onion and fennel bulb and cook, stirring, just until the onion is translucent but not colored, about 5 minutes. Add the rice, season with salt and pepper and cook, still stirring, about 5 minutes more.   Add 1 cup of the hot stock. Cook, stirring often, until the rice absorbs most of the liquid. Add another cup of the hot stock and cook and stir as before.   Continue cooking, stirring regularly and adding the stock 1 cup at a time, until 6 cups of stock have been added.   At this point, taste the rice. Usually, the rice will need another 1/2 to 1 cup stock and a few more minutes to cook.

4.   Stir in the fennel-parsley purée, the cheeses, fennel seeds and Pastis. Taste and season with salt and pepper. Refrigerate until cold.

5.   With your hands, a spoon or a small ice cream scoop, form balls 3/4- to 1-inch in diameter. Using your thumb, make a deep indentation in the center of each ball. Fill with 1/4 teaspoon piquillo pepper coulis, pinch the edges together to enclose the filling and quickly roll between your palms to re-shape. Roll each ball in the all-purpose flour, then in the eggs, and finally in the bread crumbs, making sure to coat evenly. Gently tap off any excess. Place the balls on a parchment paper-lined baking sheet and freeze for at least 2 hours.

6.   Pour 3 to 4 inches of peanut oil into a deep pot or casserole and heat until it reaches 325°F, measured by a deep-fat thermometer. Fry the balls in batches until golden brown, 2 to 3 minutes for each batch. Using a slotted spoon, carefully lift the balls out of the oil and onto a plate lined with a double thickness of paper towels. Pat off any excess oil and season with salt. Serve immediately.

Wine selection
- Grüner Veltliner Kamptal (Austria)
  Hirsch-Kammerner Heiligenstein 1999

"" Dry yet round, this wine's aromas of peach kernel and white flowers
are reserved but lingering. The wine has a mineral accent that
amplifies the fennel and a nice zesty finish that complements
the crust of the risotto. ""

What I love about catering in the Bellecour Banquet Room at Daniel is orchestrating every detail to make a very successful party—creating the menu and choosing the wine to be in harmony with the celebration. —DB

Dungeness Crab Salad with Avocado & Grapefruit Gelee

Makes 4 appetizer servings

For the Grapefruit Gelée:
- 3 1/2 two-gram gelatin sheets
- 2 cups fresh pink grapefruit juice (from about 3 large Ruby Red grapefruits)
- 1 tablespoon grenadine syrup

1. In a small bowl of cold water, soften the gelatin sheets. Lift the gelatin out of the water and squeeze it gently to remove excess moisture.
2. Prepare an ice-water bath in a large bowl and set aside. In a medium saucepan, bring 1/2 cup of the juice to a boil. Remove the pan from the heat. Add the softened gelatin sheets and stir to dissolve. Mix in the remaining juice and grenadine. Transfer the mixture to a medium bowl, place in the ice-water bath and stir until the liquid becomes syrupy.

For the Dungeness Crab:
- 16 cups water
- 1 tablespoon salt
- 1 onion, peeled and cut into large chunks
- 1 carrot, scrubbed and cut into large chunks
- 1 stalk celery, washed and cut into large chunks
- 1 lemon, scrubbed and cut into quarters
- 1 clove garlic, peeled and crushed
- One 1-inch piece fresh ginger, peeled and sliced
- 1/2 stalk lemongrass, ends trimmed and tough outer leaves removed, crushed
- Spice sachet (10 sprigs cilantro, 1 bay leaf, 1 star anise, 1/2 teaspoon coriander seeds, 1/2 teaspoon whole black peppercorns, and 1/2 teaspoon fennel seeds, tied in cheesecloth)
- Two 2- to 2 1/2-pound Dungeness crabs

1. In a large stockpot, bring the water, salt, onion, carrot, celery, lemon, garlic, ginger, lemongrass and spice sachet to a boil. Add the crabs and cook for 40 minutes. Transfer the crabs to a large bowl. Strain the poaching liquid through a fine-mesh sieve over the crabs and let the crabs cool to room temperature in the poaching liquid.
2. When cool enough to handle, remove the back shell of each crab. Remove and discard the viscera and the feather gills from the body section. Rinse the crab thoroughly under cold running water. Break the crab in half to obtain two sections with the legs attached. Separate the legs from each other, leav-ing a portion of the body attached to each leg for easy handling. Crack the shell of each of the claws, legs and the body and remove the meat. Discard the shells and refrigerate the crabmeat until ready to use.

For the Mayonnaise:
- 1 large egg yolk
- 1 teaspoon freshly squeezed lemon juice
- 1 teaspoon Dijon mustard
- 1/2 teaspoon sherry vinegar
- Salt and freshly ground white pepper
- 1/2 cup vegetable oil

Working in a medium bowl, whisk together the egg yolk, lemon juice, mustard and vinegar; season with salt and pepper. Whisking constantly, drizzle in the vegetable oil. Start by adding the oil in droplets and when the mixture starts to look thick and creamy, pour the oil into the bowl in a slow, steady stream. Refrigerate until ready to use.

For the Avocado:
- 2 large very ripe avocados, halved, pitted, peeled and cut into 1/4-inch dice
- 2 tablespoons extra-virgin olive oil
- 1 tablespoon freshly squeezed lemon juice
- 10 sprigs cilantro, leaves only, thinly sliced
- Pinch of sugar
- Dash of Tabasco
- Salt and freshly ground pepper

In a medium bowl, toss together the avocado, oil, lemon juice, cilantro, sugar and Tabasco. Season with salt and pepper.

To Serve:
- 1/2 Ruby Red grapefruit
- 10 sprigs cilantro, leaves only, thinly sliced
- Salt and freshly ground pepper
- Sprigs of dill

1. Cut the peel and white pith from the grapefruit. Working over a medium bowl, cut between the membranes to release the segments. Cut the segments into 1/4-inch dice.
2. Toss together the crab meat, half of the mayonnaise, and cilantro. Season with salt and pepper.
3. Place 3 small spoonfuls of the seasoned avocado on each dinner plate. Place 3 large spoonfuls of the grapefruit gelée around the avocado. Place the crab meat over the avocado and grapefruit gelée, scatter the diced grapefruit around and garnish with dill sprigs. Serve immediately.

Wine selection
- Marlborough Sauvignon Blanc (New Zealand) Cloudy Bay 2001

" The exotic fruit aromas in this light Sauvignon Blanc perfectly echo the grapefruit in the dish while not hiding the delicate flavors of the crab. "

Black Truffle Crusted Cod with Braised Endives

Makes 4 servings

For the Black Truffle Crust:
- 6 tablespoons unsalted butter, softened
- 1 ounce fresh black truffles, finely chopped
- 1/2 cup fresh white bread crumbs
- 1 tablespoon chopped savory
- Salt and freshly ground pepper

In a medium bowl, mix together the butter, truffles, bread crumbs, savory, salt and pepper. Between two pieces of parchment paper, roll out the butter mixture to form an 8-inch square approximately 1/8-inch thick. Place the truffle butter packet in the freezer for at least 30 minutes. Remove from the freezer and cut the packet into 4 equal squares; keep refrigerated until needed.

For the Sauce:
- 1 cup unsalted beef stock or store-bought low-sodium beef broth
- 1 tablespoon finely chopped truffle
- 1 teaspoon sherry vinegar
- 1 tablespoon unsalted butter
- Salt and freshly ground pepper

In a small saucepan over medium-high heat, bring the stock to a boil and reduce to 1/2 cup. Add the truffle and vinegar and, over high heat, reduce the liquid by half. Stir in the butter and season with salt and pepper. Set aside and keep warm.

For the Braised Endives:
- 2 tablespoons unsalted butter
- 8 medium Belgian endives, cut lengthwise in half, cored and cut into very thin strips
- Juice of 1 lemon
- 1/2 cup heavy cream
- Salt and freshly ground pepper

Warm the butter in a large sauté pan over medium-high heat. Add the endive and cook until a light golden brown. Add the lemon juice, heavy cream, salt and pepper, reduce the heat to medium and cook, while stirring, until the endive is tender and the cream has reduced to about 2 tablespoons, 12 to 15 minutes. Set aside and keep warm.

For the Cod:
- 1 tablespoon extra-virgin olive oil
- Four 6-ounce center-cut cod fillets, skin left on
- Salt and freshly ground pepper
- 1 clove garlic, peeled and lightly crushed
- 1 sprig thyme
- 1 tablespoon unsalted butter
- Black Truffle Crust (from above)

1. Center a rack in the oven and preheat the oven to 350°F.
2. Warm the olive oil in a large ovenproof skillet over medium-high heat. Season the fillets with salt and pepper and slip them into the pan, skin side down, along with the garlic and thyme. Sear the fish for 4 minutes on one side and turn over. Place the pan in the oven and cook for 4 minutes. Add the butter and roast for 1 minute longer, basting the fish with the butter, until the fillets are nicely glazed. The fish should be opaque, moist and lightly firm when pressed. Remove the pan from the oven.
3. Preheat the broiler.
4. Place a truffle-butter packet over each fillet. Place the pan under the broiler and watch the fillets closely until the tops are golden brown, about 4 minutes. Remove the pan from the oven and serve immediately.

To Serve
- Fresh black truffles, thinly sliced

Divide the endive evenly among four warm dinner plates. Place the cod fillets over the endive and spoon the sauce around the plate. Garnish with the black truffle slices.

Wine selection
- Beaune 1er Cru "Grèves" (France) Domaine Jacques Prieur 1997

"The delicate texture of the cod and the earthy, yet elegant, preparation calls for a Pinot Noir of a higher pedigree. This '97 (A lighter vintage drinking well today) from Jacques Prieur is an understated wine with notes of cherry and roasted nuts."

Cote de Boeuf Rossini

Makes 4 servings

For the Vegetables:
- 8 small California carrots, peeled and trimmed
- 8 spring onions, white part with 1/2-inch of green only
- 4 green Romano beans, trimmed and halved
- 2 tablespoons unsalted butter
- 12 small Yukon Gold potatoes (approximately 3 pounds), peeled and halved
- 2 cloves garlic, peeled and halved
- 12 large fresh porcini or wild mushrooms (approximately 1 pound), trimmed, cleaned and cut into 1/4-inch thick slices
- 1 sprig thyme
- Salt and freshly ground pepper

1. Bring a large pot of salted water to a boil. Add the carrots. After 3 minutes add the onions. After 1 minute add the beans and blanch until the vegetables are tender, about 5 minutes. Drain and set aside.
2. Center a rack in the oven and preheat the oven to 350°F.
3. Melt the butter in a Dutch oven or large casserole over medium-high heat. Add the carrots, onions, potatoes, garlic, mushrooms and thyme and cook until the butter is foamy. Place the pan in the oven and bake for 25 minutes. Add the beans, cover the pan with a lid and bake for 25 minutes, continuously basting the vegetables with the pan juices. Remove the thyme. Season with salt and pepper. Set aside and keep warm.

For the Sauce, Foie Gras and Beef:
- 2 tablespoons extra-virgin olive oil
- 1/2 pound beef stew meat, cut into 2-inch cubes
- Salt and freshly ground pepper
- 2 1/2 teaspoons whole black peppercorns, crushed
- 2 shallots, peeled and thinly sliced
- 1/4 cup cognac or brandy
- 1 cup unsalted beef stock or store-bought low-sodium beef broth
- 1/2 cup truffle juice
- 1 small bunch Italian parsley, stems and leaves separated
- 2 ounces fresh black truffles, cleaned and cut into 1/4-inch thick slices
- 1 pound fresh foie gras, denerved and

deveined and cut into 1/2-inch thick slices
- 2 bone-in beef rib-eye chops (about 1 1/2 pounds each)
- 4 tablespoons (1/2 stick) unsalted butter
- 2 cloves garlic, peeled and halved
- 2 sprigs thyme

1. Warm the oil in a large nonstick sauté pan or skillet over high heat. Season the beef cubes with salt and pepper. When the pan is hot, slip the beef into the pan. Cook, turning as needed, until the cubes are well browned on all sides. Reduce the heat to medium, add 1/2 teaspoon of the pepper and the shallots and cook, stirring, for 10 minutes. Deglaze with the cognac and cook until the liquid has almost evaporated. Add the beef stock, truffle juice and parsley stems and reduce the liquid by one-third to one-half. Strain the sauce through a fine-mesh sieve. Immediately toss the truffles into the strained sauce and season with salt and pepper, if necessary.
2. Season the foie gras slices with salt and pepper. Set a large, heavy sauté pan over high heat and sauté the foie gras slices until golden brown, 3 to 4 minutes on each side. Drain the foie gras on a plate lined with paper towels. Set aside and keep warm.
3. Center a rack in the oven and preheat the oven to 350°F.
4. Season the chops with salt. Sprinkle the remaining 2 teaspoons of pepper over both sides of the chops, pressing the pepper into the meat. In a large ovenproof sauté pan or skillet, warm 3 tablespoons of the butter over high heat. When the pan is hot, add the chops and cook for 8 minutes. Turn the chops over and cook for another 8 minutes. Reduce the heat to medium and add the remaining 1 tablespoon butter, the garlic and the thyme. Place the pan in the oven and cook for another 5 minutes while continually basting the meat. Transfer the meat to a plate and let rest for 5 minutes.

To Serve:
If necessary, rewarm the vegetables. Place the chops on the center of a large platter. Arrange the vegetables around the meat. Arrange the foie gras slices down the center of the rib-eye. Using a slotted spoon, remove the truffle slices from the sauce and arrange the slices down the center of the foie gras. Garnish with the parsley leaves and serve the sauce separately.

Wine selection
- Napa Valley Cabernet Sauvignon (U.S.) Araujo "Eisele Vineyard" 1995

"The Eisele vineyard near Calistoga, provides the grapes for this classically styled Napa Valley Cabernet. It is rich with spicy and dark berry aromas. The wine coats the palate, providing a perfect foil for the meat. It also has a backbone of firm, sweet tannins that cut nicely through the foie gras."

Baked Apple Tart with Hazelnut Biscuit & Ginger Ice Cream

Makes 6 servings

For the Ginger Ice Cream:
- 2 cups whole milk
- 1/2 cup heavy cream
- 1/4 cup powdered milk
- One 3-inch piece fresh ginger, peeled and thinly sliced
- 1 vanilla bean, split and scraped
- 1 cup sugar
- 4 large egg yolks

1. In a medium saucepan over high heat, combine the milk, cream, powdered milk, ginger and vanilla bean pod and seeds, and bring to a boil. Remove from the heat, cove, and infuse for 15 minutes. Strain through a fine-mesh sieve into a clean pot and return to a boil. Set aside.

2. Prepare an ice-water bath in a large bowl and set aside. In a medium bowl, whisk together the sugar and egg yolks until light and pale. Gradually pour half the hot milk mixture over the yolks while whisking constantly. Pour the mixture back into the saucepan. Cook over medium heat, stirring constantly with a wooden spoon, until the mixture thickens and coats the back of the spoon, 3 to 4 minutes. Strain through a fine-mesh sieve into a medium, heatproof bowl. Place in the ice-water bath and cool completely.

3. Using an ice cream maker, process the ice cream according to the manufacturer's instructions. Place in a covered container and freeze for at least 1 hour before serving.

Wine selection
- Monbazillac (France)
  Château Tirecul-La Gravière 1998

66 Scents of tropical fruit, lychee and new oak dominate this rich dessert wine from the southwest of France, making it a good match for the ginger and ice cream. The acidity of the apples slightly tames the sweetness of the wine. 99

For the Baked Apples:
- 6 Gala apples, peeled and cored
- 1/4 cup sugar
- 3/4 cup freshly squeezed orange juice
- 3 tablespoons unsalted butter
- 2 vanilla beans, split and scraped

1. Center a rack in the oven and preheat the oven to 300°F.
2. Cut the apples in half. Place cut side down and slice the apples 1/4-inch thick. Keep the slices together to maintain the apples' shape. Place the sliced apple halves, cut side down, in a 9- by 11-inch baking dish. The apples should be tightly packed. Sprinkle the apples with the sugar and pour the orange juice over the apples. Dot the apples with the butter and vanilla bean seeds and place the vanilla bean pods in the dish.
3. Cover the pan with aluminum foil and bake until the apples are soft but still hold their shape, about 1 hour.

For the Hazelnut Financier:
- 4 tablespoons (1/2 stick) unsalted butter
- 3 large egg whites
- 1/3 cup sugar
- 1/2 cup hazelnut flour
- 1/4 cup plus 1 tablespoon all-purpose flour
- 1/4 cup almond flour
- 1 tablespoon honey

1. In a small saucepan or skillet, cook the butter over medium heat until light brown. Set aside and cool completely.
2. In a medium bowl using a wire whisk, whip the egg whites to soft peaks. Using a wooden spoon, gradually stir in the brown butter, sugar, hazelnut flour, all-purpose flour, almond flour and honey, mixing well after each addition. Refrigerate the batter at least 3 hours or overnight.

To Assemble the Tarts:
1. Center a rack in the oven and preheat the oven to 400°F. Place six 4-inch nonstick tart pans on a baking sheet.
2. Arrange the apples in a circular pattern in overlapping layers in the tart pans until three-fourths full, about 1 apple per pan. Using the back of a spoon, firmly press down on the apples. Using a pastry bag fitted with a 1/2-inch round tip, fill the bag with the financier batter. Starting in the center of each tart pan, pipe a continuous pinwheel pattern covering the apples, leaving a 1/2-inch border around the edge of the tart pan uncovered.
3. Bake until the financiers are dark brown, about 20 minutes, rotating the pans halfway through baking. (The batter may bake over the edges slightly.) Run a knife around the edges of the pans and invert the tarts onto serving plates.

Serve warm topped with a scoop of the ginger ice cream.

Dinner Service
There's nothing more exciting in cooking than the pressure of service. The most exhilarating thing for a chef is to push himself to new limits, to juggle ten new tasks at once and to stay focused with the precision and speed required. —DB

7:00 p.m.

Daniel
Tasting Menu

For Him

ROASTED FOIE GRAS
with port, figs and frisée

PEEKY TOE CRAB SALAD
with coriander and cumin in a carrot coulis

ROAST SEA SCALLOPS
with bean fricassee and pistou broth

STEAMED STRIPED BASS
with chanterelles and lettuce cream

ROASTED SWEETBREADS
with green spring vegetables

**MARROW AND PORCINI CRUSTED PAVÉ OF
FILET MIGNON**
with parsley mashed potatoes

CHEESE COURSE
with cherry marmalade

BANANA CHOCOLATE TART
*with macadamia nougat and butterscotch rum
ice cream*

For Her

RHUBARB TERRINE AND FOIE GRAS
with fleur de sel

TUNA TARTARE
*with sevruga caviar, cucumber and lemon
coulis*

OPEN LOBSTER RAVIOLI
with pea purée

HALIBUT BRAISED IN OLIVE OIL
*with leeks, hon shimeji mushrooms
and a sorrel emulsion*

ROASTED SQUAB
*with foie gras, peppered apricots, spinach
and turnip confit*

STUFFED SADDLE OF LAMB
*with chanterelles, swiss chard, pine nuts
and tomato confit*

CHEESE COURSE
with sauterne-poached apricots

STRAWBERRY MELBA
with lime chantilly

Roasted Foie Gras with Port, Figs & Frisée

Makes 6 appetizer servings

For the Frisée Salad:
- 2 cups frisée (1 head), white and light yellow parts only, trimmed
- 2 tablespoons extra-virgin olive oil
- 1 teaspoon sherry vinegar
- 1 tablespoon sliced almonds, lightly toasted and coarsely chopped
- Salt and freshly ground pepper

In a medium bowl, toss the frisée with the oil, vinegar and almonds. Season with salt and pepper and set aside.

For the Port Sauce and Figs:
- 1 1/2 cups port
- 1 small stalk lemongrass, tough outer leaves removed, crushed and sliced
- 12 ripe Black Mission figs
- Salt and freshly ground pepper

In a medium saucepan, bring the port, lemon grass and figs to a boil. Reduce the heat to medium-low and simmer, while basting and turning the figs frequently, until the liquid has reduced to 1/4 cup, approximately 15 minutes. Using a slotted spoon, remove the figs from the pan. Season the sauce with salt and pepper. Strain the sauce through a fine-mesh sieve. Keep warm and set aside.

For the Foie Gras:
- 1 1/2 pounds (1 lobe) fresh foie gras, denerved, deveined and cut into 12 pieces
- Salt and freshly ground pepper

Season the foie gras with salt and pepper. Set a large heavy sauté pan over high heat and sauté the foie gras slices for 3 minutes on each side. Drain the foie gras on a plate lined with paper towels.

To Serve:
Place 2 slices of foie gras in the center of each warm plate. Top with a small mound of frisée salad. Drizzle the port sauce around and garnish each plate with 2 figs.

Rhubarb & Foie Gras Terrine with Fleur de Sel

Makes 1 terrine

- 2 pounds foie gras, denerved and deveined
- 1/2 tablespoon fine sea salt
- 1/2 teaspoon freshly ground white pepper
- 1/2 teaspoon sel rose
- 1 tablespoon cognac
- 1 lime
- 1 lemon
- 1 orange
- 6 stalks rhubarb, peeled, trimmed and cut in half
- One 1 1/2-inch piece peeled ginger
- 1/2 stalk lemongrass, tough outer leaves removed, crushed
- 3/4 cup sugar
- 8 cups water
- 1 tablespoon grenadine

1. Put the foie gras in a shallow container and sprinkle evenly with the salt, pepper, sel rose and cognac. Cover with plastic wrap, pressing the wrap directly against the surface of the foie gras, and refrigerate for 4 hours.

2. Center a rack in a convection oven and preheat the oven to 285°F. Place a porcelain terrine mold (10 inches long by 3 1/2 inches wide at the top, 3 1/2 inches deep and 9 inches long and 2 1/2 inches wide at the bottom) on a jelly roll pan or in a roasting pan with sides that are at least 1 inch high.

3. Remove the foie gras from the refrigerator and bring to room temperature. Press the foie gras into the terrine mold and place in the oven. Bake for 35 minutes and then remove from the oven. If your terrine does not come with a top, cut a piece of styrofoam or thick cardboard to fit just inside the terrine and wrap the styrofoam or cardboard well in plastic wrap. Set into the terrine and then weight it down with heavy cans (maximum weight should be 3 to 4 pounds). Refrigerate for at least 12 hours.

4. Finely grate the zest of half the lime; juice the whole lime. Repeat with the lemon and orange. Place a wire rack over a jelly roll pan. Combine the citrus zests and juices, rhubarb, ginger, lemongrass, sugar, water and grenadine and bring to a boil. Reduce the heat to medium and simmer until the rhubarb is tender but still holds its shape, 6 to 10 minutes. Make sure not to let the rhubarb get too soft. Remove the rhubarb and let cool on the wire rack. Cut the rhubarb into logs that are 3/8-inch thick and as long as possible.

TASTING MENU

DISHES 16
COURSES 9
WINES 9

Wine selection
- Macon-Cléssé "Cuvée Botrytis du 14 October" (France) Domaine Jean Thevenet

"This is a rare example of Chardonnay harvested late with some botrytis ("noble rot," like in a Sauternes) by one of the most talented winemakers in France. The wine is rich with quince and roasted-nut aromas and leaves some sweetness on the palate."

5. Remove the terrine from the refrigerator and remove the cans and top. Scrape up any fat that has accumulated on the pan or on the top of the terrine, and transfer it to a small saucepan. Warm over low heat just to melt the fat and then remove from the heat.

6. Unmold the terrine and, using a very hot knife, carefully cut the foie gras lengthwise into 2 equal slices. Wash and dry the mold and line with plastic wrap, allowing the plastic to extend over the sides of the mold. Put the bottom slice back into the mold facing the same way it was originally. Pour 2 tablespoons of melted fat over the foie gras and smooth with the back of a spoon. Place the rhubarb logs lengthwise on top, keeping them close together and touching. Spoon 2 more tablespoons of fat on top and smooth with the back of the spoon. Press the second slice of foie gras back into the mold. Weight down as before and return to the refrigerator for at least 12 hours.

To Serve:
- Fleur de sel
- Toasted slices of bread

Unmold the terrine and cut into 1/2-inch thick slices. Place one slice of foie gras terrine on each chilled dinner plate and sprinkle with fleur de sel. Serve immediately with toasted bread.

Tuna Tartare with Sevruga Caviar, Cucumber & Lemon Coulis

Makes 4 appetizer servings

For the Lemon Coulis (makes 1/2 cup):
- 6 lemons (use Meyer lemons if they are in season)
- 1 cup water
- Pinch of saffron threads
- 1 tablespoon sugar
- 2 teaspoons salt
- 1/4 cup grapeseed oil
- Salt and freshly ground white pepper

1. Using a vegetable peeler, remove the zest from the lemons, being careful not to remove the white pith below the skin. Squeeze 2 tablespoons of juice from the lemons and reserve. Place the zest in a small pot and add enough cold water to cover. Bring to a boil over high heat. Drain the zest and repeat the process 4 times.

2. In a small pot over high heat, combine the lemon zest, water, saffron, sugar and salt and bring to a boil. Reduce to a simmer and cook until the zest is tender, 5 to 7 minutes. Drain and reserve the liquid.

3. Place the lemon zest, juice and oil in a blender; purée until smooth. Transfer to a small bowl. If the coulis is too thick, add the reserved poaching liquid as needed. Season with salt and pepper. Cover and refrigerate.

For the Cucumber Coulis (makes 1/3 cup):
- 1 tablespoon extra-virgin olive oil
- 2 tablespoons chopped white onion
- 1/2 shallot, peeled, trimmed and sliced
- 1 tablespoon chopped celery
- 1/2 small English cucumber, diced
- 2 tablespoons finely diced, peeled Idaho potatoes
- 3/4 cup unsalted chicken stock or store-bought low-sodium chicken broth, plus additional if needed
- 2 sprigs Italian parsley, leaves only
- Salt and freshly ground pepper

1. Heat the olive oil in a medium sauté pan over medium heat. Add the onion, shallots and celery and cook, stirring frequently, until the vegetables are tender but have no color, about 5 minutes. Add the cucumber, potato and enough chicken stock to cover. Cook until the potato is tender, 8 to 10 minutes. Add the parsley during the last minute of cooking. Season with salt and pepper.

2. Transfer the vegetable mixture to a blender and purée until smooth, stopping occasionally to scrape down the sides of the blender. Transfer to a small bowl and season with salt and pepper. Cover and refrigerate.

For the Cucumber Slices:
- 2 small English cucumbers

Using a mandoline, thinly slice the cucumbers lengthwise. Trim each slice into a 4- by 1 1/2-inch rectangle. Wrap with damp paper towels and refrigerate until ready to use.

For the Radishes:
- 2 watermelon radishes or 4 red radishes, trimmed

Using a mandoline, thinly slice the radishes into paper thin rounds; cut each in half. Wrap with damp paper towels and refrigerate until ready to use.

For the Tuna Tartare:
- 1 lemon
- 12 ounces sushi-quality tuna loin, cut into 1/4-inch dice
- 2 tablespoons extra-virgin olive oil
- 1 tablespoon finely chopped chives
- 2 teaspoons grated fresh wasabi or horseradish
- Salt and freshly ground pepper

Finely grate the zest of the lemon. Cut the lemon in half;

squeeze enough juice to equal 1 tablespoon. In a medium bowl, mix together the lemon zest and juice, tuna, olive oil, chives and wasabi. Season with salt and pepper.

To Serve:
- 4 ounces Sevruga caviar

In the center of each chilled dinner plate place 3 cucumber slices so they form a 4-inch square. Using a 2 1/2- by 1 1/2-inch ring mold centered on the cucumber square, fill with one-quarter of the tuna tartare. Gently press down on the tartare. Top with an even layer of caviar Remove the ring mold and press the radish slices, round side up, around the outside of the tuna, slightly overlapping the slices. Drizzle the lemon and cucumber coulis around the plate or serve on the side. Serve immediately.

Peeky Toe Crab Salad with Coriander & Cumin in a Carrot Coulis

Makes 4 appetizer servings

For the Carrot Coulis:
- 2 teaspoons extra-virgin olive oil
- 2 large carrots, peeled, trimmed and thinly sliced
- 1/4 cup thinly sliced onions
- 1/3 stalk celery, peeled, trimmed and thinly sliced
- 1/4 medium leek, white part only, thinly sliced
- Spice sachet (1/4 teaspoon each of fennel seeds, coriander seeds, cumin seeds, whole white peppercorns, finely chopped Italian parsley leaves, and 1 pinch of crushed red pepper, tied in cheesecloth)
- 3 cups unsalted chicken stock or store-bought low-sodium chicken broth
- 3/4 cup carrot juice, homemade or store-bought, strained
- Juice of 1 lime
- Salt and freshly ground pepper
- Tabasco sauce

1.   Warm the oil in a large sauté pan over low heat. Add the carrot, onion, celery and leek and cook very slowly, stirring, until the vegetables soften but do not color, 15 to 20 minutes. Add the sachet and enough chicken stock to cover the carrots. Bring to a boil, lower the heat and simmer until the stock reduces to nearly dry, approximately 30 minutes. Discard the spice sachet.
2.   Using a blender, hand-held immersion blender or food processor and working in batches, purée the vegetables until very smooth. Allow the purée to cool. Measure the purée, add an equal amount of fresh carrot juice and blend thoroughly. Add more juice, if needed, until the consistency is such that the sauce coats the back of a spoon. Season the sauce with the lime juice, salt, pepper and 2 drops of Tabasco sauce.

For the Cumin-Coriander Mousseline:
Note: This makes much more than needed but can be reserved for another use.

- 1 teaspoon cumin seeds
- 2 teaspoons coriander seeds
- 1 large egg yolk
- 2 teaspoons freshly squeezed lemon juice
- 1 teaspoon Dijon mustard
- 1/2 teaspoon sherry vinegar
- Salt and freshly ground white pepper
- 1/2 cup vegetable oil
- 1/2 small clove garlic, peeled and finely chopped
- 2 cups heavy cream

1.   In a small sauté pan over medium heat, toast the cumin and coriander seeds separately, swirling the pan, until fragrant, about 4 minutes. Place the two spices in a spice grinder and process until finely ground.
2.   Working in a medium bowl, whisk together the egg yolk, lemon juice, mustard and vinegar; season with salt and pepper. Whisking constantly, drizzle in the vegetable oil. Start by adding the oil by droplets and when the mixture starts to look thick and creamy, pour the oil into the bowl in a slow, steady stream. Fold in the remaining ingredients, taste the mousseline sauce and add more salt and pepper, if needed. If you think the mousseline is too thick, stir in a splash of lemon juice or water.

For the Crab and Salad:
- 1 pound Maine Peeky Toe or other best-quality fresh crabmeat
- 3 tablespoons extra-virgin olive oil
- 1 tablespoon freshly squeezed lemon juice
- Salt and freshly ground pepper
- 1 small head frisée, white part only

Toss the crabmeat very gently (you don't want to crush or shred it) with a little of the olive oil and lemon juice to taste and season with salt and pepper. Repeat with the frisée.

To Serve:
Spoon 2 to 3 tablespoons of carrot coulis in the center of each shallow soup plate and, using the back of a spoon, spread the coulis into a 3-inch circle. Place a 2 3/4-inch ring mold in the center of the coulis. Divide the crab meat among the molds and top each with a small spoonful of mousseline. Carefully remove the ring. Garnish with a bouquet of frisée and serve immediately.

Wine selection
- Traminer Aromatico "Vallagarina" (Italy) La Cadalora 2000

"Coriander, a dominant flavor, meshes very well with the rose petal aromas of Gewurztraminer. This wine from north-eastern Italy is bone dry and lets the crab's texture shine through."

Roasted Sea Scallops with Bean Fricassee & Pistou Broth

Makes 4 appetizer servings

For the Pistou Sauce (makes 1 cup):

The pistou can be made a day ahead of time and kept covered in the refrigerator. Bring to room temperature and stir before using. Extra sauce can be tossed with pasta or spread on toasted croutons or sandwiches. Store in an airtight container, refrigerated, for 1 week or freeze up to 1 month.

- 2 bunches basil (about 8 ounces), leaves only
- 1/2 clove garlic, peeled
- 1 teaspoon pine nuts, lightly toasted
- 1 teaspoon grated Parmesan cheese
- 1/2 cup extra-virgin olive oil

1.   Bring a medium pot of salted water to a boil. Plunge the basil into the boiling water and blanch for 2 minutes. Drain the leaves and run under cold water to stop the cooking process. Drain and squeeze the leaves of excess water.

2.   Put all the ingredients in the bowl of a food processor fitted with the steel blade attachment. Process until smooth, about 2 minutes. Transfer to a bowl, press a piece of plastic wrap against the surface and set aside.

For the Bean Fricassee:

- 1/4 pound Romano beans, trimmed and cut into 1-inch segments
- 1/4 pound wax beans, trimmed and cut into 1-inch segments
- 1/4 pound haricot verts, trimmed and cut into 1-inch segments
- 1 tablespoon extra-virgin olive oil
- 8 pearl onions, peeled and quartered
- 1/2 cup unsalted chicken stock or store-bought low-sodium chicken broth
- 1 clove garlic, peeled and finely chopped
- 1 tablespoon unsalted butter
- 1 medium beefsteak tomato, peeled, seeded and cut into 1/4-inch dice
- 1 tablespoon finely chopped basil leaves
- 1 tablespoon finely chopped Italian parsley leaves
- 1 tablespoon 1/4-inch diced lemon segments
- 2 tablespoons pitted and finely chopped kalamata olives
- 1 tablespoon sliced almonds
- Salt and freshly ground pepper

1.   Fill a medium bowl halfway with an ice-water bath and set aside. Bring a large pot of salted water to a boil. Add the Romano and wax beans and cook for 5 minutes. Add the haricot verts and cook until the beans are tender, 5 to 7 minutes. Using a mesh strainer, remove the beans and place in the ice-water bath to cool. Drain and set aside.

2.   Warm the olive oil in a large sauté pan over medium heat. Add the onions and cook, while stirring, until translucent, 3 to 5 minutes. Add the chicken stock and reduce by half. Add the cooked beans, garlic and butter and cook until the beans are lightly glazed. Add the tomato, basil, parsley, lemon, olives and almonds and cook until heated through, about 1 minute. Season with salt and pepper and keep warm.

For the Roasted Sea Scallops:

- 6 tablespoons Japanese rice flakes
- 2 large eggs
- 1 tablespoon all-purpose flour
- Salt and freshly ground pepper
- 8 large sea scallops
- 1 tablespoon extra-virgin olive oil
- 1 tablespoon unsalted butter

1.   Place the rice flakes on a small plate and set aside. In a small bowl, mix together the eggs, flour and a pinch each of salt and pepper. Season the scallops with salt and pepper. Dip one side of each scallop into the egg mixture and then into the rice flakes.

2.   Warm the olive oil in a medium nonstick sauté pan over medium heat. Add the scallops, crust side down, and cook for 2 minutes. Add the butter and continue to cook until golden brown, about 2 more minutes, being careful not to burn the rice flakes. Turn the scallops over and cook for another 2 minutes.

To Serve:

- 1/2 cup unsalted chicken stock or store-bought low-sodium chicken broth
- 1/2 cup Pistou Sauce (see recipe above)
- Salt and freshly ground pepper

In a small saucepan, combine the chicken stock and pistou over medium-high heat and bring to a boil. Season with salt and pepper. Divide the fricassee between four shallow soup bowls. Place the scallops on top, spoon more fricassee on the scallops and drizzle the pistou sauce around the vegetables.

Wine selection
- Napa Valley Sauvignon Blanc (U.S.) Mason 2000

66 The zesty acidity in this Napa Valley Sauvignon offers a nice counterpoint to the richness of the sauce while the mineral touch of the wine echoes the texture of the lobster. 99

207

Open Lobster Ravioli & Pea Puree

Makes 4 appetizer servings

For the Ravioli Dough:

- 1 cup soft wheat flour, type 00
- 1 large egg yolk
- 1 large egg
- 1/2 tablespoon extra-virgin olive oil
- 1/4 teaspoon salt
- All-purpose flour

1. In a bowl, mix together the flour, egg yolk, egg, oil and salt by hand. Transfer to a floured work surface and knead the dough until smooth and elastic, 4 to 5 minutes. Wrap in plastic wrap and let rest in the refrigerator for at least 2 hours or overnight.

2. Line a baking sheet or jelly-roll pan with parchment paper and lightly dust with flour.

3. Remove the ravioli dough from the refrigerator and unwrap. Flatten the dough into a 3- by 4-inch rectangle. Pass the dough through a pasta machine until thin enough to see your hand through. Using a 5-inch round cutter, cut out 8 circles and place them on the prepared baking sheet. Cover the ravioli with plastic wrap and refrigerate. Discard the dough scraps.

For the Lobster Bisque:
- Two 1 1/2-pound live lobsters
- 1 tablespoon extra-virgin olive oil
- 1/4 cup carrots, cut into 1/4-inch dice
- 1/2 cup onions, cut into 1/4-inch dice
- 1/4 cup celery, cut into 1/4-inch dice
- 1/4 fennel, cut into 1/4-inch dice
- 1/2 head of garlic
- 1 sprig thyme
- 1/2 bay leaf
- Salt and freshly ground pepper
- 1 1/2 tablespoons tomato paste
- 1/2 pound plum tomatoes, quartered
- 1 tablespoon cognac or brandy
- 1/2 cup dry white wine
- 4 cups unsalted chicken stock or store-bought low-sodium chicken broth
- 1/2 cup heavy cream

1. Rinse the lobsters under cold water. Bring a large stock pot of water to a boil and plunge the lobsters into the water. Boil for 3 minutes and remove. Cut the tails from the heads and claws and return the tails to the boiling water for 4 minutes more. In the meantime, hold the heads and claws under cold running water to cool. Drain the tails, let cool and remove the shells. Cut each tail in half, devein if necessary and reserve. Separate the heads, claws and legs. Remove and discard the feathery gills from the body, and all other innards, reserving only the dark green coral (which may have turned light orange during the 3 minutes of boiling) for use at the end of the recipe. Roughly chop the tail carcasses, heads and claws (including the claw meat).

2. In a large shallow pot, heat the oil over high heat and add the lobster carcasses, heads and claws. Cook for 5 minutes, reduce the heat slightly, and add the claw meat, carrot, onion, celery, fennel, garlic, thyme and bay leaf. Season with salt and pepper and sweat, without color, until the vegetables are translucent, 8 to 10 minutes. Add the tomato paste, stir for 3 minutes, and add the fresh tomatoes. Add the cognac and flambé. When the flame has died out, add the white wine and cook until reduced by half. Add the chicken stock, bring to a boil, and simmer until the liquid is reduced by half, 50 to 60 minutes.

3. Remove the lobster carcasses, garlic, thyme and bay leaf and discard. In a small bowl, whisk together the lobster coral and heavy cream, add to the soup and cook, stirring, until the coral turns bright orange, approximately 3 minutes. Using a blender or food processor and working in batches, purée the soup until smooth. Strain through a fine-mesh sieve. Adjust for seasoning with salt and pepper, if needed. Keep warm.

For the Vegetables and Pea Purée:
- 6 ounces snow peas, trimmed
- 1/4 pound English peas, shelled (1 1/2 cups)
- 2 tablespoons extra-virgin olive oil
- Salt and freshly ground pepper
- 1 tablespoon unsalted chicken stock or store-bought low-sodium chicken broth

1. Prepare an ice-water bath in a small bowl and set aside. Bring a pot of salted water to a boil. Plunge the snow peas into the pot and cook for 3 minutes. Transfer the English peas to a colander, plunge the colander into the pot with the snow peas and cook for another 5 minutes. Remove the colander and hold the English peas under cold running water to cool. Transfer the snow peas to the prepared ice-water bath. Once cooled, drain the snow peas and set aside with 1/2 cup of the English peas. In a food processor or blender, purée the remaining 1 cup English peas with 1 tablespoon of the olive oil and enough water to make a very thick yet smooth purée. Season with salt and pepper, set aside and keep warm.

2. Warm the remaining 1 tablespoon olive oil in a large sauté pan. Add the snow peas, the remaining 1/2 cup English peas and the stock, and cook, basting the vegetables, until tender, 3 to 4 minutes. Season with salt and pepper.

To Serve:
- 2 sprigs tarragon, leaves only

1. Bring a large pot of salted water to a boil. Add the ravioli and cook until almost al dente, about 2 minutes. Gently remove the ravioli with a mesh strainer and toss them gently in a pan with 1 1/2 cups of the lobster bisque and the reserved lobster tails over medium heat for a few minutes. Taste and season with salt and pepper.

2. Spoon some of the remaining bisque into four warm soup bowls and top with a ravioli round. Place the pea purée, vegetables and lobster tail over the ravioli. Top with a ravioli round, spoon some more bisque over the ravioli and garnish with fresh tarragon leaves.

Wine selection
- Napa Valley Sauvignon Blanc (U.S.) Mason 2000

"The zesty acidity in this Napa Valley Sauvignon offers a nice counterpoint to the richness of the sauce while the mineral touch of the wine echoes the texture of the lobster."

Steamed Striped Bass with Chanterelles & Lettuce Cream

Makes 4 servings

For the Garnish:
- 2 shallots, peeled
- Cooking oil for frying

1. Using a mandoline or a very sharp chef's knife, cut the shallots into thin slices. Wash and pat dry.

2. Pour 1 to 2 inches of oil into a small pot and heat the oil to 325°F as measured on a deep-fat thermometer. Fry the shallots until golden brown, 3 to 5 minutes, and drain them on a plate lined with a double thickness of paper towels.

For the Lettuce Cream:
- 1 head Boston lettuce
- 1 tablespoon extra-virgin olive oil
- Salt and freshly ground pepper

1. Remove and reserve 4 large outer leaves of the lettuce for the fish. Remove the core from the lettuce head.

2. Prepare an ice-water bath in a medium bowl and set aside. Bring a large pot of salted water to a boil. Add the lettuce to the boiling water and blanch for 2 minutes. Remove from the heat, drain and transfer to the prepared ice-water bath. Once cooled, drain and gently squeeze the excess moisture from the lettuce.

3. Place the olive oil and lettuce into a blender and purée until smooth. If the cream is too thick, add some water to thin. Season with salt and pepper. Set aside and keep warm.

For the Chanterelle Sauce:
- 1 tablespoon plus 1 teaspoon unsalted butter
- 1/2 pound chanterelle mushrooms, trimmed, cleaned and cut into 1/2-inch pieces
- 1 cup unsalted beef stock or store-bought low-sodium beef broth
- Salt and freshly ground pepper

Melt 1 tablespoon of the butter in a large sauté pan over high heat. Add the mushrooms and cook, while stirring, until the water from the pan has almost completely evaporated. Add the stock and continue to cook until the liquid is reduced by half. Stir in the remaining 1 teaspoon butter and season with salt and pepper. Set aside and keep warm.

For the Vegetables:
- 2 tablespoons unsalted butter
- 1 pound baby turnips, peeled, greens trimmed to 1/2-inch and cut lengthwise into 1/8-inch thick slices
- 2 cups unsalted chicken stock or store-bought low-sodium chicken broth
- 2 cloves garlic, peeled and crushed
- 2 sprigs thyme
- Salt and freshly ground pepper
- 4 heads baby romaine lettuce, outer leaves removed
- 1 tablespoon extra-virgin olive oil

1. Melt the butter in a large sauté pan over medium-high heat. Add the turnips, chicken stock, 1 of the garlic cloves and 1 thyme sprig and cook, while stirring and basting the turnips frequently, until tender and nicely glazed, 8 to 10 minutes. Season with salt and pepper. Set aside and keep warm.

2. Center a rack in the oven and preheat the oven to 350°F.

3. Cut off and discard the bottom 2 inches of each head of romaine. Warm the olive oil in an ovenproof sauté pan or casserole over medium heat. Add the lettuce, the remaining garlic clove and thyme and season with salt and pepper. Cover with aluminum foil, slide the pan into the oven and bake until the lettuce is tender, 5 to 7 minutes. Set aside and keep warm.

For the Fish:
- Four 6-ounce center-cut striped bass fillets, skin removed and cut into rectangular pieces
- Salt and freshly ground pepper
- Reserved 4 Boston lettuce leaves

Season the fish with salt and pepper. Bring a small amount of water to a boil in the bottom of a steamer (a wok with a bamboo steamer, a fish poacher or a stockpot with a steaming rack is ideal). Place the fillets on the steamer tray, making sure that the fish does not come into contact with the boiling water, cover and steam for 6 minutes. Cover the fillets with the lettuce leaves and steam for an additional 2 minutes, until the fish is opaque, moist and lightly firm when pressed. Remove the tray from the steamer.

To Serve:
Divide the turnips evenly among four warm dinner plates. Spoon the chanterelle sauce around the turnips. Place the fish over the turnips and top with the baby romaine. Garnish with the fried shallots and drizzle the lettuce cream around the chanterelle sauce. Serve immediately

Halibut Braised in Olive Oil with Leeks & Hon Shimeji Mushrooms

Makes 4 servings

For the Sorrel Sauce:
- 1 egg in the shell
- 1 bunch sorrel, leaves only
- 1/2 cup peanut oil
- 5 ice cubes

1. Bring a small pot of water to a boil. Gently slip in the egg and cook for 4 minutes. Remove the egg from the pot and let the egg cool under cold running water for 2 minutes. Gently peel the egg.
2. In a blender, whirl together the soft-poached egg, sorrel leaves, oil and ice cubes until smooth. Set aside until needed.

For the Vegetables:
- 2 tablespoons unsalted butter
- 4 stalks celery, cut into 3-inch segments and thinly sliced lengthwise
- 2 leeks, white and light green parts only, thinly sliced lengthwise
- 1/2 cup heavy cream
- Salt and freshly ground black pepper
- 1 pound Yukon Gold potatoes, peeled and cut into 1/4-inch thick slices
- 1 clove garlic, peeled and crushed
- 1 sprig thyme
- 2 cups unsalted chicken stock or store-bought low-sodium chicken broth
- Sorrel sauce (from recipe above)

1. Melt 1 tablespoon of the butter in a large sauté pan over medium heat. Add the celery and leeks and cook, while stirring, for 2 minutes. Add the heavy cream and continue to cook until the vegetables are tender and the cream has reduced to 2 tablespoons, about 10 minutes. Season with salt and pepper. Transfer the vegetables to a plate and keep warm.
2. Wipe the inside of the sauté pan clean with a paper towel; melt the remaining 1 tablespoon butter over medium-high heat. Arrange the potatoes in an even layer and top with the garlic, thyme and stock; cook until the potatoes are tender, about 10 minutes. Using a slotted spoon, transfer the potatoes to a plate and keep warm. Combine the Sorrel Sauce with any remaining liquid in the pan. If there is not enough liquid or the sauce is still too thick, add some water or chicken stock to thin. Season with salt and pepper. Set aside and keep warm.

For the Halibut and Mushrooms:
- 4 ounces Hon Shimeji (beech) mushrooms
- Four 6-ounce center-cut halibut fillets, bone and skin removed
- Salt and freshly ground pepper
- 2 cups extra-virgin olive oil
- 1 clove garlic, peeled and crushed
- 1 sprig thyme

1. Center a rack in the oven and preheat the oven to 350°F.
2. Trim the mushroom bases to separate the stems. Pull apart all the mushrooms.
3. Season the fish with salt and pepper. Heat the olive oil in a Dutch oven or large casserole to 200°F as measured on a deep-fat thermometer. Slip in the fish, mushrooms, garlic and thyme. Loosely cover with aluminum foil, slide the pan into the oven and bake for 8 minutes. Using a slotted spoon, carefully lift the fish and mushrooms out of the oil and onto a plate lined with a double thickness of paper towels. Pat off any excess oil and season with salt and pepper, if necessary.

To Serve:
Reheat the vegetables, potatoes and sorrel sauce, if necessary. Divide evenly among four warm dinner plates. Top each with a halibut fillet and garnish with the Hon Shimeji mushrooms. Spoon the sorrel sauce around the plates.

Wine selection
- Santa Maria Valley Pinot Gris/Pinot Blanc, California (U.S.)
  Au Bon Climat "Cuvée Hildegard" 1999

“ This cuvée made according to traditional Burgundian wine-making customs has a floral nose with citrus tones that stand up to the lettuce cream. The wine has great acidity and volume in the mouth, teaming up very well with the moist mild tasting fish. ”

Roasted Sweetbreads with Green Spring Vegetables

Makes 4 servings

For the Vegetables:
- 3 tablespoons unsalted butter
- 2 small zucchini
- 8 stalks asparagus, peeled, trimmed and cut into 1/2-inch segments
- 3 ounces haricot verts, tipped
- 3 ounces snow peas, trimmed
- 1/2 pound sugar snap peas
- 4 scallions, white part only
- 1/2 cup heavy cream
- 1 cup unsalted chicken stock or store-bought low-sodium chicken broth
- Salt and freshly ground pepper

1. In a small sauté pan, cook 2 tablespoons of the butter over medium-high heat until light golden brown. Set aside.

2. Cut off the ends of the zucchini and slice lengthwise in half. Using a teaspoon, scoop out the seeds and cut into 1/2-inch thick slices.

3. Bring a large pot of salted water to a boil. Toss in the asparagus, haricot verts and snow peas. Put the snap peas in a colander, plunge the colander into the pot and cook for 5 minutes. Add the zucchini and scallions and cook for another 2 minutes. Remove the colander, leaving the snap peas in it; turn the other vegetables into a sieve and hold all the ingredients under cold running water to cool them down quickly and to set their colors; drain again. Set aside half of the snap peas.

4. In a blender or food processor, purée the reserved snap peas with the brown butter. Strain the purée through a fine-mesh sieve. Set aside.

5. In the bowl of a mixer fitted with the whisk attachment or by hand using a whisk, whip the cream until medium peaks form. Set aside in the refrigerator until needed.

6. In a small saucepan, bring the chicken stock to a boil over high heat and reduce by half.

7. Melt the remaining 1 tablespoon butter in a large sauté pan

over medium-high heat. Add the blanched vegetables and reduced stock; cook until the vegetables are heated through. Right before serving, fold the pea purée and the whipped cream together and gently stir into the vegetables. Season with salt and pepper.

For the Sweetbreads:
- 2 pounds sweetbreads
- 2 tablespoons extra-virgin olive oil
- Salt and freshly ground pepper
- 2 tablespoons unsalted butter
- 5 spring onions, white part with 1/2 inch of green only
- 2 cloves garlic, peeled
- 1 sprig thyme
- 1/4 cup cognac or brandy
- 1 1/2 cups unsalted beef stock or store-bought low-sodium beef broth

1. Bring a large pot of salted water to a boil. Add the sweetbreads and blanch for 2 to 3 minutes. Place the sweetbreads in a bowl of cold water and refrigerate at least 5 to 6 hours or overnight. Drain and remove the outer membrane of the sweetbreads.

2. Warm the olive oil in a Dutch oven or casserole over medium-high heat. Season the sweetbreads with salt and pepper and add to the pan. Cook, turning as needed, until the sweetbreads are well browned on all sides. Reduce the heat to medium and add the butter, onions, garlic and thyme. Continue to cook, stirring and scraping the bottom of the pan, until the onions begin to caramelize and the sweetbreads are firm, approximately 15 minutes. Deglaze with the brandy, add the stock and cook until the liquid is reduced by half. Taste and season with salt and pepper, if necessary. Transfer the sweetbreads to a cutting board and cut into 1/2-inch thick slices.

To Serve:

Place a small mound of the vegetables on the center of each warm dinner plate. Top with slices of the sweetbreads and spoon the pan sauce around. Serve immediately.

Roasted Squab with Foie Gras, Peppered Apricots, Spinach & Turnip Confit

Makes 4 servings

For the Apricots:
- 8 ripe apricots, cut in half and pitted, 4 pits crushed and reserved
- 3 tablespoons honey
- 1 tablespoon freshly squeezed lemon juice
- 1/4 teaspoon cracked black pepper

1. Center a rack in the oven and preheat the oven to 350°F.

2. Butter a 9-inch square baking pan. Place the apricots, cut side up, in the pan. Drizzle with the honey and lemon juice and sprinkle with the pepper. Slide the pan into the oven and bake until the apricots are tender, approximately 10 to 15 minutes depending on the ripeness of the apricots. Remove and set aside.

For the Vegetables:
- 3 tablespoons unsalted butter
- 12 baby turnips, peeled and greens trimmed to 1/2 inch
- 1 cup unsalted chicken stock or store-bought low-sodium chicken broth
- Salt and freshly ground pepper
- 1/2 pound spinach, stems and tough center veins removed
- 1 clove garlic, peeled and crushed

1. Melt 2 tablespoons of the butter in a large sauté pan over medium-high heat. Add the turnips and cook for 2 to 3 minutes. Add the chicken stock, cover the pan and cook until the turnips are tender, approximately 10 minutes. Season with salt and pepper. Transfer the turnips to a plate and keep warm.
2. Wipe the pan clean with a paper towel. Melt the remaining 1 tablespoon butter in the same pan over high heat. Add the spinach and garlic and season to taste with salt and pepper. Toss until the spinach is tender but still bright green, about 5 minutes. Discard the garlic and drain off any liquid remaining in the pan. Set aside and keep warm.

For the Squab:
- Four 3/4 pound squabs
- 1/4 teaspoon coriander seeds
- 1/4 teaspoon freshly grated nutmeg
- 1/4 teaspoon Thai peppercorns, crushed
- 4 ounces crème fraîche
- 1 tablespoon extra-virgin olive oil
- 1 tablespoon unsalted butter
- 1 shallot, peeled, trimmed and finely chopped
- 1/2 teaspoon cracked black pepper
- 8 roasted apricot halves (from recipe above)
- Reserved crushed apricot pits (from recipe above)
- 2 tablespoons brandy
- 1 tablespoon amaretto

- 2 cups unsalted chicken stock or store-bought low-sodium chicken broth

1. Remove the wing joints, legs and breasts from the squab. De-bone the thighs and the legs. Reserve all the livers and the carcasses.
2. In a spice grinder, crush together the coriander seeds, nutmeg and Thai peppercorns. Combine the spices and crème fraîche. Spread the mixture over the breasts and marinate overnight in the refrigerator.
3. Place a rack in the top position of the oven and preheat the broiler.
4. Wrap the thighs in aluminum foil. Place the marinated squab breasts and thighs on the rack of the broiler pan and broil the breasts 3 minutes on each side until the skin is golden brown. Remove from the oven. Let the squabs rest for 5 minutes.
5. Cut the reserved carcasses into small pieces. Warm the olive oil in a medium sauté pan over medium-high heat. Add the carcasses and the reserved livers. Reduce the heat to medium and add the butter, shallots and cracked pepper. Cook until the shallot is tender and has no color, 10 to 12 minutes. Add the apricot halves and the crushed pits and continue to cook, while stirring, until the apricots become a little bit mushy. Deglaze with the brandy and amaretto and cook until the liquid is reduced by half. Add the chicken stock and simmer for 30 minutes. Strain the sauce through a fine-mesh sieve, taste and season with salt if necessary. Set aside and keep warm.

For the Foie Gras:
- 1/2 pound fresh foie gras, denerved and deveined and cut into four pieces
- Salt and freshly ground pepper

Season the foie gras with salt and pepper. Set a heavy sauté pan over high heat and sear the foie gras for 2 to 3 minutes on each side.

To Serve:
- Rock salt

If necessary, reheat the spinach and turnips. In a 375°F oven, reheat the squab breasts, if necessary, for 2 minutes on each side. Cut each breast in half. Place a mound of spinach on the center of each warm dinner plate. Arrange the squab breast and two legs on top along with a piece of foie gras. Season the meat with rock salt. Drizzle the sauce and scatter the apricots and turnips around the plate. Serve immediately.

Wine selection
- Volnay 1er Cru Ancienne Cuvée Carnot "Caillerets" (France) Bouchard Père & Fils 1997

66 This soft Pinot Noir from one of the most fabled wine villages in the world has crushed berry and spice aromas and a velvet texture that works well with both the sweetbreads and the squab. 99

213

Stuffed Saddle of Lamb with Chanterelles, Swiss Chard, Pine Nuts & Tomato Confit

Makes 4 servings

For the Stuffed Saddle of Lamb:

- 6 tablespoons extra-virgin olive oil
- 1 tablespoon chopped onion
- 3 ounces chanterelles, trimmed
- 1 pound Swiss chard, stems and tough center ribs removed, cut into thin strips
- 1/2 clove garlic, peeled and finely chopped
- Salt and freshly ground pepper
- 4 pieces tomato confit
- 1 tablespoon pine nuts, coarsely chopped
- 1 side saddle of lamb (Ask the butcher to remove all excess fat, the long flat flank sections and the bone, which the butcher should cut into 1-inch segments and reserve)
- 2 tablespoons unsalted butter

1. Warm 1 tablespoon of the olive oil in a large sauté pan over medium-high heat. Add the onion and cook, while stirring, until tender but colorless. Add the chanterelles and cook for 3 minutes. Add the Swiss chard and garlic, season with salt and cook, while stirring, until tender, about 5 minutes. Add the tomato confit and pine nuts and toss all the ingredients together. Season with salt and pepper; cool. When the vegetables are cool enough to handle, squeeze out all excess water.

2. Center a rack in the oven and preheat the oven to 350°F.

3. Spread the lamb saddle on a work surface and butterfly to a 1-inch thickness. Season both sides with salt and pepper. Spoon the Swiss chard stuffing down the length of the saddle in a compact log, then roll the meat up tightly around the stuffing. Tie the lamb at 1-inch intervals with kitchen twine.

1. Put a pot of salted water up to a boil. Plunge the asparagus into the boiling water and cook at a steady simmer until they can be pierced easily with the tip of a knife, 3 to 4 minutes for regular asparagus and 6 to 7 minutes for jumbo. Gently lift the asparagus out of the pot and hold under cold running water to stop the cooking and set the color. When cool, pat dry between kitchen towels. Cut each stalk in half on the diagonal.

2. Melt the butter over medium-high heat and cook to a light golden brown. Reduce the heat to medium. Add the potatoes and rosemary and season with salt and pepper. Cook for 10 minutes, while stirring and basting the potatoes. Add the carrots and cook for 10 minutes more, while stirring and basting the vegetables. Add the mushrooms and cook until the vegetables are tender, about 3 minutes. Toss in the asparagus and cook until warm. Taste and season with salt and pepper, if necessary.

For the Sauce:
- 1 cup extra-virgin olive oil
- Reserved saddle bone (from above)
- 2 tomatoes, cut in half
- 1 carrot, peeled and trimmed
- 1/2 head of garlic
- Bouquet garni (4 sprigs chervil, 4 sprigs Italian parsley, 1 bay leaf, 1 sprig thyme and 6 black peppercorns, tied in cheesecloth)
- 1 sprig rosemary
- 1/2 bay leaf
- 1 cup dry white wine
- 1 cup unsalted beef stock or store-bought low-sodium beef broth
- 2 tablespoons unsalted butter
- Salt and freshly ground pepper

Warm the olive oil in a large sauté pan over high heat. Add the bones and roast for 20 minutes, while stirring. Add the tomatoes, carrot, garlic, bouquet garni, rosemary and bay leaf and cook for 7 minutes. Deglaze with the white wine and cook until the liquid in the pan has almost evaporated. Add the beef stock and reduce by half. Strain through a fine-mesh sieve. Return the strained sauce to the pan and stir in the butter until melted. Season with salt and pepper.

To Serve: Remove the string from the saddle and cut into 8 slices. Divide the vegetables among four warm dinner plates. Place 2 stuffed saddle slices on top of the vegetables. Spoon the sauce around.

4. Warm the remaining 5 tablespoons oil in a roasting pan over medium-high heat. When the oil is hot, add the saddle to the pan and sear until golden brown, 8 to 10 minutes, turning the saddle as needed. Remove the saddle from the pan, wrap in aluminum foil and return to the roasting pan. Add the butter to the pan, slide the pan into the oven and roast for 8 minutes, basting occasionally. Give the saddle a half-turn and roast for 7 minutes more. When done, the internal temperature of the saddle should reach 150°F on an instant-read thermometer. Transfer the lamb to a warm plate and let rest for 7 minutes.

For the Vegetables:
- 8 stalks asparagus, peeled and trimmed
- 2 tablespoons unsalted butter
- 1 pound small Fingerling potatoes
- 1/2 sprig rosemary
- Salt and freshly ground pepper
- 4 California carrots, peeled, trimmed and cut in half on the diagonal
- 3 ounces chanterelle mushrooms, trimmed

Wine selection
- Napa Valley Cabernet Sauvignon (U.S.) Provenance 1999

 Provenance is a structured Cabernet with firm tannins that mesh nicely with the richness of the filet mignon. The marrow crust only adds to the extravagant dark berry aromas of the wine. **99**

Marrow & Porcini Crusted Pave of Filet Mignon with Mashed Potatoes

Makes 4 servings

For the Marrow and Porcini Crust:

- 3 ounces beef marrow (removed from about 1 pound marrow bones)
- Salt
- 2 tablespoons extra-virgin olive oil
- 1/2 pound porcini mushrooms, trimmed and sliced 1/8-inch thick
- 1 clove garlic, peeled and crushed
- 1 sprig thyme
- 1/4 teaspoon whole black peppercorns, crushed
- 3 tablespoons unsalted butter
- 1/2 cup plus 2 tablespoons fresh bread crumbs

1. One day ahead, put the marrow in a bowl with enough water to cover generously. Add 2 teaspoons salt, cover the bowl and soak overnight in the refrigerator, changing the water and adding 2 teaspoons more salt several times during this period.

2. In a medium saucepan, bring 1 quart salted water to a boil. Remove the marrow from its soaking liquid and cut into 1/4-inch cubes. Drop the cubes into the boiling water and count 30 to 45 seconds before lifting the marrow out of the water with a slotted spoon. Put the marrow on a plate and set aside.

3. Warm the oil in a large sauté pan over medium-high heat. Add the mushrooms, garlic, thyme and peppercorns. Cook until all the water from the mushrooms has evaporated and they are golden brown, approximately 7 to 8 minutes. Discard the garlic and thyme and let the mushrooms cool. When cool, finely chop the mushrooms.

4. Melt the butter in a small saucepan; cook until light golden brown. Mix together the marrow, mushrooms, brown butter and bread crumbs. Between two pieces of parchment paper, roll out the marrow mixture to form a 6-inch square approximately 1/4-inch thick. Wrap the pack in plastic wrap and freeze for at least 30 minutes. Remove from the freezer and cut the packet into four equal squares; keep refrigerated until needed.

For the Parsley Mashed Potatoes:
- 1 small bunch Italian parsley, leaves only
- 1/4 cup water
- 3 cloves garlic, peeled and halved
- 1 3/4 pounds Idaho potatoes, peeled and cut into quarters
- 1 cup whole milk, warmed
- 6 tablespoons unsalted butter
- Salt and freshly ground pepper

1. Prepare an ice-water bath in a small bowl and set aside. Bring a small pot of salted water to a boil. Toss in the parsley leaves and cook until tender, 3 to 5 minutes. Drain and transfer to the prepared ice-water bath. When cool, drain and squeeze the leaves of excess water. Put the parsley leaves and water into a blender and purée until smooth. Set aside.

2. Place the garlic in a small saucepan and add enough cold water to cover. Bring to a boil over high heat. Drain and repeat the process two more times. Drain and set aside.

3. Put the potatoes in a pot of cold salted water and bring to a boil. Cook until the potatoes can be pierced easily with a knife. Drain the potatoes, then put them back into the pot and, shaking the pot constantly over medium heat, heat the potatoes just enough to cook off the excess moisture. While the potatoes are still hot, purée them with the blanched garlic in a food mill or potato ricer.

4. In a small pot, bring the milk and butter to a boil. Stir the milk and parsley purée into the potatoes until well combined; season with salt and pepper. Set aside and keep warm.

For the Salad:
- 8 celery leaves
- 8 Italian parsley leaves
- 1 porcini mushroom, trimmed and thinly sliced
- 1 teaspoon extra-virgin olive oil
- Squeeze of fresh lemon juice
- Salt and freshly ground pepper

Toss together all the ingredients.

For the Filet Mignon:
- 2 tablespoons unsalted butter
- Four 8-ounce filet mignons
- 4 cloves garlic, peeled and halved
- 2 sprigs thyme
- 1/2 cup dry red wine
- 1 cup unsalted beef stock or store-bought low sodium beef broth
- Salt and freshly ground pepper
- Porcini and Marrow Crust (from above)

1. Melt the butter in a large sauté pan or skillet over medium high heat. Add the beef, garlic and thyme and cook for 8 minutes. Flip the beef over and cook for another 8 minutes. Transfer the filets to the rack of a broiler pan and keep warm. Pour in the red wine and, stirring and scraping the bottom of the pan, cook until almost all of the liquid has evaporated. Add the beef stock and reduce by half. Season with salt and pepper. Set the sauce aside and keep warm.

2. Preheat the broiler.

3. Put a porcini-marrow square over each filet and place under the broiler until the tops are golden brown, about 4 minutes—watch them closely. Pull the pan from the oven and serve immediately.

To Serve:
Place a small mound of parsley mashed potatoes on the center of each warm dinner plate and top with a filet. Garnish with the salad and spoon the sauce around.

Wine selection
- Napa Valley Cabernet Sauvignon (U.S.) Provenance 1999

66 Provenance is a structured Cabernet with firm tannins that mesh nicely with the richness of the filet mignon. The marrow crust only adds to the extravagant dark berry aromas of the wine. 99

Cherry Marmalade

For the Hard & Blue-Veined Cheeses
Makes about 1 cup

- 1 lemon
- 1 pound fresh dark cherries, pitted
- 1 vanilla bean, split and scraped
- 2 tablespoons honey
- One 3-inch cinnamon stick
- 1 spice sachet (1 tablespoon whole black peppercorns and 2 cloves, tied in a cheesecloth)
- 1 teaspoon cornstarch
- 2 tablespoons Kirsch

Finely grate the zest of half of the lemon; juice the whole lemon. In a small saucepan over medium-high heat, combine the lemon zest and juice, cherries, vanilla bean, honey, cinnamon stick and spice sachet and bring to a boil. Reduce the heat, cover, and simmer, while stirring occasionally, until the cherries are tender, 10 to 15 minutes. Stir together the cornstarch and Kirsch until blended and slowly stir into the cherries. Cook until the mixture thickens and turns translucent, about 30 seconds. Remove the spice sachet and cinnamon and refrigerate until cold.

Sauterne-Poached Apricots

For the Soft-Ripened, Washed-Rind & Goat Milk Cheeses
Makes about 1 cup

- 1/2 pound dry apricots (approximately 1 cup)
- 3/4 cup Sauterne
- 1 bay leaf
- 1 cinnamon stick
- 2 teaspoons whole black peppercorns, crushed and tied in cheesecloth
- 1/2 sprig rosemary

Place the apricots, Sauterne, bay leaf, cinnamon stick, black peppercorns and rosemary in the top of a double boiler. Cover the top tightly with plastic wrap and steam the apricots for 30 to 40 minutes until tender. Discard the bay leaf, cinnamon stick, black peppercorns and rosemary. Refrigerate the apricots in an airtight container overnight. Drain and bring the apricots to room temperature before serving.

Wine selection
- Priorat (Spain)
  Dolc de l'Obac 2000

1. Hard Cheese

- A. Two-year-old Gruyère, Fribourg, Switzerland
- B. Two-year-old Mimolette,
  Nord-pas-de-Calais, France
- C. Comté, millésime 2000,
  Franche-Comté, France

2. Soft-Ripened Cheese and Washed-Rind Cheese

- A. Camembert, Normandy, France
- B. Livarot, Normandy, France
- C. Brillat Savarin, Normandy, France
- D. Pont l'Evèque, Normandy, France
- E. Epoisses, Burgundy, France
- F. Aged Robiola, Lombardy, Italy

3. Goat Milk Cheese

- A. Bonne Bouche, Vermont, United States
- B. Crottin de Chavignol, Berry, France
- C. Pouligny St. Pierre, Berry, France
- D. Chevrot, Poitou-Charentes, France
- E. Selles sur Cher, Berry, France
- F. Vacherin de chèvre, Ariège, France
- G. Valençay, Berry, France

4. Blue-Veined Cheese

- A. Roquefort, Auvergne, France
- B. Bleu de Termignon, Savoie, France
- C. Fourme d'Ambert, Auvergne, France
- D. Rochebaron, Auvergne, France
- E. Persillé de Champsaur, Hautes Alpes, France
- F. Persillé de Malzieu, Lozère, France

Strawberry Melba with Lime Chantilly

Makes 8 servings

For the Lime Gelée (makes 1 1/3 cup):
- 6 or 7 limes
- Three 2-gram gelatin sheets
- 1/3 cup plus 2 tablespoons water
- 1/2 cup sugar

1. Finely grate the zest of 2 of the limes and then squeeze enough juice to equal 3/4 cup plus 2 tablespoons.
2. Soften the gelatin sheets in a small bowl of cold water. Lift the gelatin out of the water and squeeze it gently to remove excess moisture.
3. In a small pot, bring the water and sugar to a boil. Remove from the heat and whisk in the lime zest and juice and the softened gelatin sheets.
4. Divide the lime juice mixture among eight 6-ounce glasses. Refrigerate until set.

For the Fromage Blanc Sorbet:
- 1/3 cup water
- 1/4 cup whole milk
- 2 tablespoons light corn syrup
- 1/4 cup plus 2 tablespoons sugar
- 1 1/4 cups fromage blanc

In a small pot, bring the water, milk, corn syrup and sugar to a boil over high heat. Whisk in the fromage blanc. Using a hand-held immersion blender, mix until smooth. Transfer to a small bowl and refrigerate. Process in an ice cream maker according to the manufacturer's instructions.

For the Strawberry Granité:
- 2 cups water
- 1/3 cup plus 1 tablespoon sugar
- 1/2 pound large strawberries, hulled and halved

1. In a small pot, bring the water and sugar to a boil. Add the strawberries. Remove the pot from the heat and cover with plastic wrap. Let the strawberries steep for 2 to 3 hours at room temperature. Using a fine-mesh sieve, strain the liquid: Do not press down on the berries. The liquid should remain clear.

2. Transfer the liquid to a loaf pan and place in the freezer. Stir occasionally with a fork until the liquid is frozen and granular.

For the Strawberry Sauce:
- 1 teaspoon sugar
- 3/4 teaspoon powdered pectin
- 3/4 cup strawberry purée

1. Combine the sugar and pectin.
2. In a small pot, bring the strawberry purée to a boil over high heat. Whisk in the sugar mixture and cook until the sugar has dissolved. Transfer to a small bowl and allow to cool. Cover and refrigerate until needed.

For the Strawberry Compote:
- 1/3 cup sugar
- 1/4 cup plus 2 tablespoons water
- 1/2 cup strawberry purée
- 1 1/2 pounds large strawberries, hulled and finely diced
- 2 vanilla beans, split and scraped

1. In a small saucepan, bring the sugar and water to a boil over high heat. Add the strawberry purée, bring to a boil and reduce to a simmer. Add the strawberries and vanilla bean seeds and cook for 2 minutes.
2. Transfer the strawberry compote to a small bowl and allow to cool. Cover and refrigerate until needed.

For the Lime Whipped Cream:
- 2 tablespoons sugar
- 1 cup heavy cream
- Finely grated zest of 1 lime
- 1/2 vanilla bean, split and scraped

Put all the ingredients in a medium bowl. Using a wire whisk, whip until medium peaks form. Cover and refrigerate until needed.

To Serve:
Place 1/4 cup of compote on top of each gelée. Place a dollop of whipped cream on top of the compote. Top with a spoonful of granité. Finish with a scoop of fromage blanc sorbet and a drizzle of sauce.

Wine selection
- Moscato d'Asti (Italy)
  La Spinetta Bricco Quaglia 2001

66 This light, slightly sparkling wine from Italy nicely cuts through the lime accented Chantilly and pairs well with the strawberries, having some red berry aromas itself. 99

Banana Chocolate Tart with Macadamia Nougat & Butterscotch Rum Ice Cream

Makes twelve 3-inch tarts

For the Chocolate Tart Shells:
- 8 tablespoons (1 stick) unsalted butter at room temperature
- 1 1/3 cups confectioners sugar, sifted
- 1 1/2 cups plus 2 tablespoons all-purpose flour
- 1/4 cup plus 3 tablespoons unsweetened cocoa powder, preferably Dutch-process, sifted
- 1 large egg, lightly beaten

1. In the bowl of an electric mixer fitted with a paddle attachment, beat the butter on medium speed until creamy. Reduce the speed to low and add the sugar, flour and cocoa, one at a time. Add the egg and mix just until the dough comes together and forms a ball. Be careful not to overmix the dough. Divide the dough in half. Shape each half into a disc and wrap the discs in plastic wrap. Refrigerate for 1 hour.

2. Butter the insides of twelve 3- by 1/2-inch rings. Place the rings on a parchment paper-lined baking sheet and set aside. On a lightly floured work surface, roll the dough to 1/8-inch thickness. Using a 4-inch round cutter, cut the dough into 6 rounds, re-rolling the scraps as needed. Press the rounds into the buttered rings, trimming any excess with a small paring knife. If the dough tears, gently press it back together with your fingertips. Refrigerate for 20 minutes. Repeat the process with the remaining disc.

3. Center a rack in the oven and preheat the oven to 350°F. Remove the tart rings from the refrigerator. Line the bottom and sides of the dough with parchment paper rounds or foil and fill with dried beans or rice. Bake for 13 to 15 minutes until the crust is firm and fully baked. Remove the parchment paper and beans. Transfer the tart shells to a wire rack, cool completely and remove the rings.

For the Caramelized Macadamia Nuts:
- 1/4 cup water
- 1/4 cup sugar
- 1 2/3 cup salted macadamia nuts, roasted and roughly chopped
- Pinch of salt

1. Center a rack in the oven and preheat the oven to 350°F. In a small saucepan over medium-high heat, combine the water and sugar. Cook just until the sugar dissolves. Set aside to cool.

2. In a medium bowl, combine the sugar syrup, macadamia nuts and salt. Spread the nuts on a parchment paper-lined baking sheet and bake until caramelized and golden brown, about 20 minutes, rotating and shaking the pan halfway through the baking process. Cool the nuts completely and store in an airtight container.

For the Butterscotch Rum Ice Cream (makes 1 1/2 pints):
- 1/4 cup packed dark brown sugar
- 1/4 cup dark corn syrup
- 2 tablespoons unsalted butter
- Pinch of salt
- 1/2 vanilla bean, split and scraped
- 1 cup heavy cream
- 1 cup whole milk
- 5 large egg yolks
- 2 tablespoons granulated sugar
- 2 tablespoons dark rum

1. Prepare the butterscotch sauce: In a small saucepan, combine the dark brown sugar, corn syrup, butter and salt and bring to a boil. Cook until the sugar dissolves, about 2 minutes.

2. Prepare an ice-water bath in a large bowl and set aside. In a small saucepan over high heat, combine the butterscotch sauce, vanilla bean pod and seeds, cream and milk; bring to a boil. Remove from the heat.

3. In a medium bowl with a wire whisk, combine the egg yolks and granulated sugar, whisking until the mixture is light and pale. Gradually pour half of the hot cream mixture over the egg mixture, whisking constantly. Pour the egg mixture back into the saucepan. Cook over medium heat, stirring constantly with a wooden spoon, until the mixture thickens just enough to coat the back of the spoon. Strain the mixture through a fine-mesh sieve into a heat-proof bowl and place in the ice-water bath; cool completely, stirring occasionally. Stir in the rum.

4. Process in an ice cream maker according to the manufacturer's instructions. Place in a covered container and freeze for at least 1 hour before serving.

For the Banana Filling:
- 2 teaspoons powdered pectin
- 2 tablespoons sugar
- 1 cup banana purée (about 2 medium)
- 2 teaspoons freshly squeezed lemon juice

1. In a small bowl, mix together the pectin and sugar.

2. In a small saucepan over high heat, bring the banana purée and lemon juice to a boil. Whisk in the sugar and pectin and bring the mixture back to a boil. Let cool to room temperature.

For the Chocolate Ganache:
- 7 ounces bittersweet chocolate, chopped
- 4 large egg yolks
- 2 large eggs
- 3 tablespoons sugar
- Pinch of salt
- 11 tablespoons (1 stick plus 3 tablespoons) unsalted butter, melted and cooled

1. Place the chocolate in a medium bowl over a pan of simmering water, making certain that the bottom of the bowl does not touch the water. Stir occasionally with a rubber spatula until the chocolate melts. Remove from the heat. (The chocolate can also be melted in a microwave oven on low power, at 10 second intervals, stirring frequently.)

Wine selection
- Tokaji Azsu (Hungary)
  Disznökö 5 Puttonyos 1995

2. In a large bowl, using a wire whisk, combine the yolks, eggs, sugar and salt. Gradually whisk in the melted chocolate until just combined. Add the melted butter, whisking slowly to prevent any air bubbles from forming. Use immediately.

To Assemble the Tarts:
1. Center a rack in the oven and preheat the oven to 350°F.
2. Place the tart shells on a parchment paper-lined baking sheet. Fill each shell halfway with the banana purée, using about 1 tablespoon. Top with the chocolate ganache, using about 2 tablespoons. Bake just until filling is set but still soft in the center, 5 to 7 minutes. The tarts can be served warm or at room temperature.

To Serve:
Serve the tarts with a scoop of butterscotch rum ice cream and garnish with the caramelized macadamia nuts.

66 The macadamian nuts in this dessert work well with the oxidized notes in this Tokaji while aromas of orange rind interlace the chocolate tart. 99

Madeleines

Makes 6 dozen small or 1 dozen large

- 3/4 cup all-purpose flour
- 1 teaspoon baking powder
- Pinch of salt
- 1/4 cup plus 2 tablespoons granulated sugar
- 2 large eggs
- 1 tablespoon honey
- 1 tablespoon packed light brown sugar
- Finely grated zest of 1 lemon
- 6 tablespoons unsalted butter, melted and kept warm
- Confectioners' sugar, for dusting

1.   In a small bowl, sift together the flour, baking powder and salt. Set aside.
2.   In a medium bowl using a wire whisk, mix the granulated sugar, eggs, honey, brown sugar and lemon zest. Add the flour mixture and whisk just until combined. Add the melted butter, stirring just until incorporated. Cover the bowl with plastic wrap and refrigerate for 1 hour.
3.   Preheat the oven to 400°F. Liberally spray either a non-stick 20-mold or 12-mold madeleine pan with nonstick cooking spray.
4.   Place the batter in a pastry bag fitted with a medium round tip. Pipe the molds two-thirds full, using about 1 teaspoon of batter for the 20-mold pan and 2 tablespoons of batter for the 12-mold pan.

5.   Bake the small madeleines until the centers rise and the edges are golden brown, about 4 minutes, rotating the pan halfway through the baking. Bake the large madeleines for 5 minutes, reduce the heat to 350°F, rotate the pan, and continue baking until the centers rise and the edges are golden brown, about 5 minutes. Remove from the oven, invert the pan and tap it against the counter to release the madeleines. Serve the madeleines warm, dusted with confectioners' sugar.

Coconut Rocher

Makes about 4 dozen rochers

- 1/2 mango, peeled and diced, or 1/4 cup mango purée
- 1 3/4 cups shredded unsweetened coconut
- 1/4 cup plus 2 tablespoons sugar
- 3 large egg whites
- 1 tablespoon unsweetened coconut milk
- Finely grated zest of 1/2 orange
- Finely grated zest of 1/2 lemon
- 3 ounces bittersweet chocolate, tempered (optional)

1.   If using fresh mango, purée the mango in a blender until smooth, adding a teaspoon or two of water, if needed.
2.   Place the mango purée, coconut, sugar, egg whites, coconut milk, and orange and lemon zests in a heatproof medium bowl. Place over a medium saucepan of simmering water,

stirring constantly with a wooden spoon until the sugar dissolves and the temperature reaches 125°F, about 4 minutes. Set aside to cool.

3. Center an oven rack and preheat the oven to 425°F. Line a baking sheet with parchment paper.

4. Fill a small bowl with warm water and set aside. Dip a small round 1/2- to 1-inch pastry tip into warm water, pack with some of the coconut mixture, and tap the mold on the counter to release the cone shaped rocher. Place the rocher, pointy end up, on the prepared baking sheet: repeat with the remaining batter. Alternatively, dip your fingers in warm water and shape about a teaspoon of the batter into a cone shape.

5. Bake until light golden brown, about 4 to 6 minutes, rotating the pan halfway through the baking process. Remove the rochers from the baking sheet and cool completely on a wire rack.

6. If desired, dip the bottom of each rocher in tempered chocolate. Let set before serving in mini-paper petit four cups.

White Chocolate Almond Nuggets

Makes about 3 dozen candies

- 1 1/2 tablespoons light corn syrup
- 1 cup slivered almonds
- 8 ounces white chocolate, finely chopped

1. Center a rack in the oven and preheat the oven to 350°F. Line a baking sheet with parchment paper.

2. In a small bowl, mix together the corn syrup and almonds until evenly coated. Spread the almonds in a single layer on the prepared baking sheet. Bake until golden brown, 5 to 7 minutes, stirring halfway through the baking process. Set aside to cool.

3. Prepare an ice-water bath in a medium bowl and set aside. Place the chopped chocolate in a small bowl. Set the bowl over a small saucepan of simmering water, making sure the bottom of the chocolate bowl does not touch the water. Stir with a rubber spatula until the chocolate melts and the temperature reaches 116°F to 118°F. Remove from the heat, place the bowl in the ice-water bath, and stir until the temperature drops to 80°F. (Make sure the chocolate does not come into contact with any water droplets.) Place the chocolate over a saucepan of warm water until the temperature reaches 85°F to 87°F. Use the tempered chocolate immediately.

4. Line a baking sheet with waxed paper or parchment paper. In a small bowl, combine the almonds and tempered chocolate until the almonds are evenly coated. Using a rounded teaspoon, place dollops of the almond mixture on the baking sheet, forming nuggets about 1 inch in diameter. If the work area is cool enough, let the chocolate set at room temperature. Otherwise place the baking sheet in the refrigerator for 10 minutes.

5. Store the nuggets in single layers between waxed paper or parchment paper in an airtight container up to 2 weeks.

Top, left to right: Jean-François Bruel (chef de cuisine at db Bistro Moderne), Daniel Boulud,
Drew Nieporent and Jean-Georges Vongerichten.

Center, left to right: Christian DeLouvrier (chef de cuisine at Lespinasse), Daniel Boulud and Jean-Louis
Dumonet (executive chef of the Carlyle Hotel).
Bottom, left to right: Mark Goldberg and Georgette Farkas.

Late-Night Chefs Dinner

This is one of the many late-night chefs dinners that I love to throw at Daniel for our local community of chefs and friends after work, after the dining room has closed down. For me these dinners are about Amitié, Fraternité and Gastromonie, which is what the French constitution would say if a chef wrote it. I always make sure there's one or two sommeliers invited so they can bring wine and I always invite one non-chef person. We have our kind of soul food, one single dish, bingo, and nothing else but a good bottle of wine. This time I chose tripe; it could have been a bouillabaisse, or a big cheese fondue party, which I also love to do. —DB

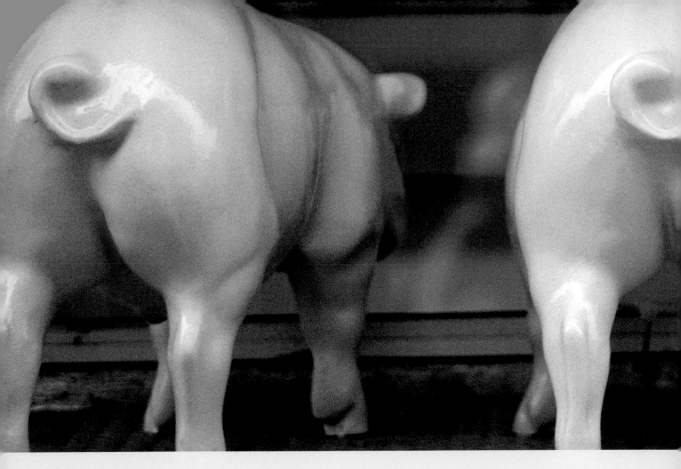

Tripes a la Mode Boulud

Makes 6 to 8 servings

For the Tripe:

- 8 pounds honeycomb calf tripe, cut into 1- by 3-inch strips and thoroughly washed
- 1/4 cup extra-virgin olive oil
- 1/4 cup cognac or brandy
- 6 onions (approximately 3 pounds), peeled, trimmed and cut into 1/2-inch-thick slices
- 8 carrots (approximately 2 pounds), peeled, trimmed and cut into 1/2-inch thick slices
- 10 stalks celery (approximately 1 pound), peeled, trimmed and cut into 1/2-inch thick slices
- 2 tablespoons chopped garlic (approximately 6 cloves)
- 3 tablespoons tomato paste
- 1 teaspoon red pepper flakes
- Two 750 ml bottles dry white wine
- 4 whole pig's feet
- 6 large tomatoes (approximately 3 pounds), peeled, seeded and cut into 1/2-inch pieces
- 1 pound Italian sausage or chorizo
- 8 cups unsalted chicken stock or store-bought low-sodium chicken broth
- Bouquet garni (3 sprigs thyme, 2 bay leaves, 1 bunch Italian parsley: stems only, leaves finely chopped and reserved, tied in cheesecloth)
- Salt and freshly ground pepper

1. Put the tripe in a large stockpot with enough cold water to cover and bring to a boil. Drain in a colander and let cool.
2. Center a rack in the oven and preheat the oven to 300°F.
3. Warm the olive oil in a Dutch oven or large casserole over high heat. Add the tripe and cook, stirring frequently, until light golden brown, about 15 to 20 minutes. Deglaze and flambé with the cognac. When the flames subside, lower the heat to medium, add the onions, carrots and celery and cook until the vegetables are tender but have no color, approximately 20 minutes.
4. Stir in the garlic, tomato paste and red pepper flakes and cook for 3 to 5 minutes. Add the white wine and reduce by half. Add the pig's feet, sausage, tomatoes, stock and bouquet garni. Season with salt and pepper. The liquid should cover the tripe by at least 3 inches. Add water or more stock, if needed. Bring the liquid to a boil. Cut out a round of parchment paper to fit inside the pot, press the paper lightly against the ingredients and bake in the oven for 4 to 5 hours. The tripe should be moist and tender and should be covered with liquid when pressed down.

For the Vegetables:

- 8 cups cold water
- 1 cup fresh or dried cranberry beans (if using dry, pre-soak the beans in cold water for 3 hours)
- 1 small onion, peeled, trimmed and chopped
- 1 small carrot, peeled, trimmed and chopped
- 2 cloves garlic, peeled and chopped
- 1 bay leaf

- 1 thyme sprig
- 8 German butterball potatoes
- 2 pounds Swiss chard, stems and tough center ribs removed

1. In a large stock pot, bring the water, cranberry beans, onion, carrot, garlic, bay leaf and thyme to a boil. Reduce the heat to medium-low and simmer the beans for 30 minutes. Add the potatoes and simmer until the beans and potatoes are tender, 20 to 30 minutes. Right before the beans and potatoes have finished cooking, season with salt. Let the beans and vegetables cool in the cooking liquid. Drain, reserve the beans and potatoes and discard the remaining vegetables and herbs.

2. Bring a large pot of salted water to a boil. Plunge the Swiss chard into the boiling water and blanch until the leaves are tender but still very green, 5 minutes. Drain the chard in a colander and hold under very cold running water. When the leaves are cool enough to handle, drain them well, then squeeze them between your hands to remove the excess moisture. Refrigerate until needed.

For the Crust:
- 1 1/2 cups fresh bread crumbs
- 2 tablespoons almond flour
- 4 tablespoons (1/2 stick) unsalted butter, softened
- 1 tablespoon chopped garlic (approximately 3 cloves)
- Reserved finely chopped Italian parsley leaves
- Salt and freshly ground pepper

Gently mix together the bread crumbs, almond flour, butter, garlic and parsley leaves. Season with salt and pepper. The mixture should be very loose. Set aside until needed.

To Serve:
- 1/4 cup kalamata olives, pitted
- 2 large tomatoes (approximately 1 pound)
- Salt and freshly ground pepper

Increase the temperature of the oven to 400°F. Remove the bouquet garni from the tripe. Transfer the pig's feet and sausage to a cutting board. Remove and discard the bones and cartilage from the pig's feet and cut the remaining meat into pieces the same size as the tripe. Cut the sausage into 1/2-inch thick pieces. Return the meat to the pot, along with the cranberry beans, potatoes, Swiss chard, olives and tomatoes. Taste and season with salt and pepper, if necessary. Scatter the crust mixture evenly over the top and bake until the crust and tripe are golden brown, 30 to 45 minutes. If the crust begins to darken, use the back of a spoon to gently press the crust down into the liquid to moisten. Serve the tripe family-style directly from the pot.

Wine selection
- Saumur "Brézé" (France)
  Clos Rougeard 1996

66 Medium bodied, round and well balanced with mineral overtones that mesh with the fatty elements in this dish, this wine, made at one of the best domaines in the Loire Valley, responds with a kick to this ultra-traditional preparation. 99

Winding Down

About seventeen hours after the first roll is baked there is a feeling that the storm has passed. The dining room is still three quarters filled but it is as if the room, the staff, the people all have taken a breath and slowed down. To be sure, there are a hundred desserts or so still to be served, a dozen parties of late comers (Europeans? Investment bankers working late? Theater-goers not satisfied with the get-em-in, get-em-out-fast ethos of Broadway dining spots, lovers ready to dine on oysters and something with truffles after a pre-dinner warm-up?).

Plenty of work remains to be done, but back in the kitchen, everyone knows it is the last lap; the crush is over. No frantic clattering, no raised-voice beehive where speed runs up against the need to be perfect. No dropped trays. No ego-shattering stares from the chef.

This is the run back to the barn. The glide in for touchdown. One by one, members of the staff wrap up their duties and change into their civvies. Time to hang out on 65th Street for a quick cigarette, then maybe a run over to 63rd Street where the sushi master of Manhattan holds court for the top chefs in town. Or the hot dog emporium on 23rd Street, or Chinatown, or the train back to the suburbs.

Since the ovens were first lit, back at 5 a.m. when Venus still hung high over the horizon, 54 kitchen staff members have poured water, wine and cocktails in 840 glasses, two hundred matchbooks have been saved as souvenirs, twelve couples have celebrated their anniversary, eight pounds of caviar and 25 pounds of foie gras have been plated and served, thirty-five pounds of butter have gone into pans or onto bread, eight diners have not been able to find anything on the menu that hit their fancy or their restricted diet so they have ordered four chopped salads, two pieces of plain broiled fish and (for a pair of finicky seven-year-old twins) two orders of spaghetti dressed with nothing more than a pat of butter and a sprinkling of parmesan cheese. Seventy bottles of wine have been ordered ranging from $39 for Willamette Valley, King Estate 1999, Pinot Gris to $863 for a magnum of Bonnes-Mares "Vieilles Vignes" Grand Cru 1988. There have been 103 individual glasses of wine poured along with five glasses of Sprite and fourteen Shirley Temples (eight by kids wanting something fancy in a cocktail glass, and the other six by designated drivers from Brooklyn Heights, Long Island, Connecticut and the wilds of New Jersey).

Daniel is ready for sushi, or maybe a trip down to NoLiTa where one of his former sous chefs has opened an interesting French-Moroccan-Asian fusion restaurant on Clinton Street. Or maybe a cigar and an Armagnac and some loud Muddy Waters CDs in his lounge with a writer friend, a couple of chefs from around town, and a group of Argentineans who, in keeping with their national style, will eat the last meals to come out of the kitchen, still amazed that Americans finish dinner when they are just getting started.

Then, after the last drink, the last joke, the last piece of food-business shop talk—and still buzzing with the juice of all that action—heads hit the pillow. In four hours the ovens will warm again and the trucks will pull into the city after the long trip from the farm. They are filled with the new day's meals-in-waiting.

Kevin Cherkas, cook at Daniel

Charlie Palmer of Aureole

Michael Romano, Union Square Café,
Mark Goldberg, Daniel Johnnes

Sushi Hatsu is a late-night hangout for chefs on the
Upper East Side. The restaurant is very classic Japanese.
Even though the chef/owner Kakuji Miyachi does not
speak a word of English, you can get great sushi at 2
a.m. here. As a joke, he's holding up two fingers in the
picture to signify that he has a two handicap in golf and
would like to play golf with me. -- DB

Odette Fada, Jean-Louis Dumonet), Christian
Delouvrier, Michael Lomanaco, Charlie Palmer, Daniel
Boulud, Jean-Georges Vongerichten, Jean-François
Bruel and Michael Romano

1:00 a.m.

Center Picture (from left to right):
Sushi Hatsu chef and owner Kakuji
Miyachi, former Daniel sous chef Olivier
Reginensi, Daniel Boulud,
Dean Santon

Guy Heksch (general manager of db
Bistro Moderne), Jessica Shapiro, Jean
Pierre Françoise (maître d'hôtel of db
Bistro Moderne) and Brett Traussi (director
of operations for the Dinex Group)

Daniel Boulud and
Jean Pierre Xiradakis

Meyer Lemon Confit

Makes 6 lemon confit

- 8 cups water
- 1/3 cup salt
- 2/3 cup sugar
- 3 cloves
- 1 cinnamon stick
- 1 tablespoon coriander seeds
- 2 teaspoons fennel seeds
- 2 star anise
- 1 bay leaf
- Pinch of saffron threads
- 6 Meyer or regular lemons

1. Combine the water, salt, sugar, cloves, cinnamon, coriander seeds, fennel seeds, star anise, bay leaf and saffron in a small pot and bring to a boil. Cut four incisions into the center of each lemon, leaving the lemon whole, and add to the pot. Simmer for 1 1/2 hours. Remove from the heat and cool.

2. When cool, remove the lemons and pat dry with paper towels. Using a small paring knife, cut the lemon into quarters and remove the zest from the bitter white pith. Discard the lemon pulp. Cut the zest according to the directions in the recipe.

(If not using the zest right away, the lemons can be stored in their poaching liquid in an airtight container for up to a month.)

Beef Stock

Makes about 2 1/2 quarts

- 1 large onion, peeled, trimmed, and halved crosswise
- 2 whole cloves
- 2 tablespoons vegetables oil
- 1 beef shank (about 6 pounds)—ask the butcher to cut it crosswise into 2-inch-thick slices, bone included, and to trim excess fat
- Salt and freshly ground white pepper
- 6 quarts water
- 6 large mushrooms, trimmed, cleaned and halved
- 4 stalks celery, trimmed and cut into 2-inch-long pieces
- 3 carrots, peeled, trimmed, and cut into 1-inch-long pieces
- 6 cloves garlic, peeled and crushed
- 5 sprigs Italian parsley
- 2 sprigs thyme
- 2 bay leaves
- 1 teaspoon coriander seeds, toasted

1. Blacken the cut sides of the onion by placing them on a very hot flat surface, such as a griddle, and let them cook until truly burnt. If you don't have a griddle, place a heavy pan over medium heat and put the onion cut side down in the pan. Cook until it is as dark as you can get it. Remove the blackened onion halves from the pan and stick a clove in each half; set aside.

2. Heat the oil in a large sauté pan or nonstick skillet over high heat. Season the meat with salt and pepper and brown the pieces a few at a time (it's important not to crowd the pan), making sure you get them really brown on all sides. As the pieces of meat are browned, transfer them to a large stockpot.

3. When all the meat is browned and in the stockpot, pour in the water, add the remaining ingredients and bring to a boil. Lower the heat to a simmer and cook for 2 hours, skimming off the foam and fat that bubbles up to the surface. Don't skimp on the skimming; it's very important to remove all the impurities and as much of the fat as you can.

4. Strain the stock through a colander and then pass it through a fine-mesh sieve. Cool to room temperature, then cover and refrigerate. (The stock can be kept, packed airtight, in the refrigerator for up to 4 days or in the freezer for up to 1 month.) When the stock is chilled, the fat will rise to the top. Before reheating the stock, spoon off and discard the fat.

Chicken Stock

Makes about 1 gallon

- 4 pounds chicken necks, backs, and wings or chicken parts, skinned, fat trimmed and rinsed
- 2 1/2 gallons cold water
- 2 medium onions, peeled, trimmed and cut into quarters
- 2 small carrots, peeled, trimmed and cut into 2-inch-long pieces
- 1 stalk celery, trimmed and cut into 2-inch long pieces
- 1 medium leek, trimmed, split lengthwise and washed
- 1/2 head garlic, split crosswise in half
- 1 bay leaf
- 5 sprigs Italian parsley
- 1 teaspoon white peppercorns

1. Put the chicken and 7 quarts of the cold water in a tall stockpot and bring to a rolling boil. Add the remaining 3 quarts water (it should be very cold) and skim off the fat that rises to the top. Adjust the heat so that the water simmers and simmer, skimming regularly, for 10 minutes.

2. Add the remaining ingredients to the pot and simmer for 3 hours, continuing to skim so that the stock will be clear. Drain the stock in a colander. Allow the solids to drain for a few minutes before discarding them, then strain the stock through a fine-mesh strainer. Cool and refrigerate. (The stock can be kept tightly covered in the refrigerator for 4 days or frozen for up to a month.)

Source Guide

All-Clad Metalcrafters
Tel: 800-ALL-CLAD
www.allclad.com
Top-quality cookware

Bernard Antony
Sundgauer Kas-Kaller
17, rue de la Montagne
Vieux-Ferrette, France 68480
Tel: (33) 3 89 40 42 22
Fax: (33) 3 89 40 31 03
French cheeses

Blue Moon Acres
P.O. Box 201
Buckingham, Pennsylvania
18912
Tel: 215-794-3093
Micro-greens and herbs

Browne Trading Co.
260 Commercial Street
Portland, ME 04101
Tel.: 800-944-7848
Fax: 207-766-2404
www.browne-trading.com
Daniel Boulud's Private Stock Caviar and Smoked Salmon, peeky toe crabmeat, crayfish, oysters, salt cod, smoked beluga sturgeon, diver and other sea scallops, and other pristine fish and seafood

Buon Italia
75 9th Avenue
New York, New York 10011
Tel: 212-633-9090
Fax: 212-633-9717
www.buonitalia.com
Specializing in Italian food products, such as 00 pasta flour, olive oil, cheese, meat

The Chef's Garden, Inc.
9009 Huron-Avery Road
Huron, Ohio 44839
Tel: 419-433-4947
www.chefs-garden.com
Finest gourmet vegetables and fruits, herbs, lettuces, edible flowers, micro-greens, exotic mushrooms, dried and fresh beans, dried and fresh fruit

Coach Farm
105 Mill Hill Road
Pine Plains, New York 12567
800-999-4628
www.coachfarm.com
Artisanal goat cheeses

D'Artagnan, Inc.
Tel: 800-DARTAGN or 973-344-0565
www.dartagnan.com
Duck-breast prosciutto, duck conifit, foie gras, partridge, guinea hen, pheasant, squab, venison, and other game, demi-glace, and wild mushrooms

De Bragga and Spitler
826-D Washington Street
New York, New York 10014
Tel: 212-924-1311
Fine-quality meats (beef, lamb, pork)

Eckerton Hill Farms
130 Far View Road
Hamburg, Pennsylvania 19526
Tel: 610-562-2591
Heirloom tomatoes and seasonal fruits and vegetables

Fancy Meats from Vermont
2604 East Hill Road
Andover, Vermont 05143
Tel: 802-875-3159
Lamb and baby pigs

Four Story Hill Farm
4C 62, Box 38
Honesdale, PA 18431
Tel: 570-224-4137
Capons, poularde, specialty-bred chickens and lamb

Fresh & Wild, Inc.
P.O. Box 2981
Vancouver, Washington 98668
Tel: 206-737-3652
Wild mushrooms

Gachot & Gachot
440 West 14th Street
New York, New York 10014
Tel: 212-675-2868
Fax: 212-243-6703
Fine meats

Gourmand, Inc.
Tel: 703-708-0000
Fax: 703-708-9393
Almond flour, chocolate, fleur de sel, sel rose, quatre épices (four-spice), sheet gelatin, piment d'espellette, puff pastry, truffles, vanilla beans, and other best-quality foodstuffs

Grace's Marketplace
1237 Third Avenue
New York, New York 10021
Tel: 212-373-0600
www.gracesmarketplace.com
High-quality produce, meats and seafood, quail eggs, piquillo peppers, pistachio oil

Hudson Valley Foie Gras
80 Brooks Road
Ferndale, New York 12734
Tel: 845-292-2500
Fax: 845-292-3009
www.hudsonvalleyfoiegras.com
Specializing in duck foie gras and duck products

Ideal Cheese Shop
942 1st Ave
New York, NY 10022
800-382-0109
www.idealcheese.com
Fine domestic and imported cheeses

In Pursuit of Tea
866-878-3832
www.inpursuitoftea.com
Fine-quality teas

International Spice House
315 West John Street
Hicksville, New York, 11802
Tel: 516-942-7248
Fax: 516-942-7249
www.spicehouseint.com
Chile peppers, Mexican oregano, Mexican ground cinnamon, spices

Jamison Farm
171 Jamison Lane
Latrobe, PA 15650

Tel: 800-237-5262
Fax: 724-837-2287
www.jamisonfarm.com
Farm-raised Pennsylvania lamb and prepared foods

J.B. Prince
36 East 31st Street, 11th Floor
New York, NY 10016
Tel: 212-683-3553
Fax: 212-683-4488
www.jbprince.com
Knives, mixers, blenders, small electrical tools, baking pans

Kalustyans
123 Lexington Avenue
New York, N.Y. 10016
Tel: 212-685-3451
Fax: 212-685-8458
www.kalustyans.com
Specializing in Middle Eastern spices and foods, as well as Japanese rice flakes, sel rose, zatar, Thai peppercorns

Keepsake Farms
9 Fishkill Farms Road
Hopewell Junction, New York 12533
Farm: 845-896-3947
Sales: 845-452-1433
www.keepsakeorchards.com
Fine fruits and vegetables

Kitchen Aid
www.kitchenaid.com
Fine-quality stand mixers

The Lobster Place, Inc.
436 West 16th Street
New York, New York 10011
Tel: 212-255-5672
www.lobsterplace.com
Fresh lobsters from Maine

L'Olivier
19 E. 76th Street
New York, New York 10021
Tel: 212-774-7676
Fax: 212-774-0058
www.lolivier.com
Florist

Millbrook Venison, Inc.
RR2 Box 133 Verbank Road
Millbrook, New York 12545
Tel: 914-677-8457
Venison and game

Mountain Sweet Farms
P.O. Box 667
Boscoe, New York 12776
Tel: 607-498-4440
Berries, beans and potatoes

M. Slavin and Sons
www.mslavin.com
Fine seafood

Murray's Cheese Shop
257 Bleecker Street
New York, New York 10014
Tel: 888-692-4339
www.murrayscheese.com
Fine domestic and imported cheeses

Patis France/Paris Gourmet
800-PASTRY-1
www.patisfrance.com
Chocolates, vanilla beans, almond flour, and other fine-quality baking ingredients

Piccinini Bros., Inc.
633 Ninth Avenue
New York, New York 10036

Tel: 212-246-8277
Fax: 212-581-7609
Classic New York butcher

Pierless Fish Corp.
www.pierlessfish.com
Fine seafood, local and imported fish and shellfish

Plantain USA
201-867-4590
Truffle juice, fresh truffles, truffle peelings

Riviera Produce Corporation
205 Jackson Street
Englewood, New Jersey 07631
Tel: 201-227-1705
Fax: 201-227-7124
Fine fruits and vegetables

F. Rozzo & Sons, Inc.
159 Ninth Avenue
New York, New York 10011
Tel: 212-242-6100
Fish and seafood

Sabatier
Customer Service: 516-794-3355
Fine-quality knives

Salumeria Biellese
378 8th Avenue
New York, New York 10001
Tel: 212-736-7376
Fax: 212-736-1093
Sausages, chorizo and charcuterie

Schaller & Weber
22-35 46th Street
Astoria, NY 11105
Tel: 800-847-4115
Fax: 718-956-9157
www.schallerweber.com
Pork belly, smoked German-style charcuterie and sausage

Sinha Trading, Inc.
120 Lexington Avenue
New York, New York 10016
Tel: 212-683-4419
Kocum, dana dal, exotic and unusual ingredients

Stone Church Farm
P.O. Box 215
Rifton, New York 12471
Tel: 914-658-3243
Squabs and free-range poultry

Sunrise Sun-Ripened Tomatoes
29 Meserole Avenue
Brooklyn, New York 11222
Tel: 212-383-2580
Tomatoes

Upstate Farms
P.O. Box 376
Red Hook, New York 12571
Tel: 845-756-3803
Fine fruits and vegetables from the Hudson Valley

Urbani Truffles USA
Tel: 718-392-5050
Fax: 718-392-1704
www.urbaniusa.com
Truffles and caviar

Vermont Quality Meat Cooperative
P.O. Box 1631
Brattleboro, Vermont 05302
Tel: 702-875-3159
Lamb and suckling pigs

Index

238